Sam has cut his teeth sharing the g[...] diverse, urban, post-Christian Austr[...] [...] enthusiasm for evangelism shines through in this practical and inspiring guide. A fantastic resource for communicating the life-changing message of Jesus to a world hungry for meaning.

> **MARK SAYERS**, author of *Reappearing Church*,
> cohost of *This Cultural Moment* podcast,
> and senior leader of Red Church

This is a delightful book and perfect for anyone who thinks evangelism is beyond their pay grade! Sam Chan motivates and equips all believers—regardless of gifting or temperament—in how to reach the hard-to-reach in today's challenging post-Christian culture. His eight tips are illuminating, thoughtful yet practical, culturally relevant, biblically faithful, and relationally effective. I loved the book, and I think you will too!

> **REBECCA MANLEY PIPPERT**, author of *Stay Salt:*
> *The World Has Changed: Our Message Must Not*

When I wasn't a Christian, I was sometimes approached by *"that* guy" who eagerly but awkwardly talked to me about Jesus. Thankfully, I ran into people who knew how not to be *"that* guy." Also thankfully, Sam Chan helps all of us to not be *"that* guy" so we can point people to the person of Jesus. Sam has taken a heavy topic and made it into a breezy read that will inform, amuse, and inspire.

> **ABDU MURRAY**, author and speaker,
> Ravi Zacharias International Ministries

Sam Chan is a breath of fresh air. His book is inspiring and practical. Challenging and kind. Timely and timeless. Strategic and genuine. He lives what he writes, yet his life and vision for effective evangelism are accessible to us all. Thank you, Sam, for this incredible gift in *How to Talk about Jesus (Without Being* That *Guy)*!

CRAIG SPRINGER, executive director,
Alpha USA, and author of *How to Follow Jesus* and *How to Revive Evangelism*

Practical, readable, and Spirit-infused! Sam Chan has given believers a pathway to sharing faith that is organic and accessible to ordinary people. Read it, put it into action, and watch God use you to share his love and grace in fresh new ways.

KEVIN HARNEY, founder of Organic Outreach International
and author of the *Organic Outreach* trilogy

Reading Sam Chan's *How to Talk about Jesus (Without Being* That *Guy* was a bit like doing a jigsaw puzzle—you have all the pieces, but you're not sure how they fit together. In terms of evangelism, I knew that things like theology, story, culture, history, and community were essential, but I hadn't grasped how they fit together until Sam gave me the code. The church owes Sam a huge debt of thanks for this excellent resource, which will help us model faithful, sustainable evangelism ourselves and also train our beloved church families to speak about Jesus.

RICO TICE, senior minister for evangelism
at All Souls Church, Langham Place,
and author of *Honest Evangelism*

In his new book, expert evangelist Sam Chan invites you into his home to see what personal evangelism looks like in his own life, complete with examples, stories, and other practical guidance. It is a great resource for every Christian who wants to help others meet Jesus.

CRAIG ELLIS, founder and CEO, The Elpis Network

Inspirational and immensely practical, Sam Chan shows us what a life of witness actually looks like—and it looks radiant! The book shines with gospel optimism and everyday wisdom. This is not about "silver bullets" (there are none!); instead Sam shows us the community, the posture, the lifestyle, and the beating heart of a witness for Jesus, earthing it in our ordinary lives of discipleship. If you're stuck thinking, *I should evangelize*, let Sam raise your gaze. This book shows us we are all witnesses, and, wonderfully, each of us can play our part.

GLEN SCRIVENER, director of Speak Life and author of *The Gift* and *3 2 1: The Story of God, the World and You*

The Jesus of the Bible *is* at work today, and finding out where he is already "unsettling" our own contacts is the most thrilling, joyful, Spirit-filled experience. What a master class from Sam "Mr. Motivator" Chan in how to get cracking. I couldn't put this book down. Thanks to Sam's engaging and oh so practical advice, many will be encouraged enough to start discovering that the power is in the *Word*, but—and it's a big but—we do have to get out to share it! When doing so, I am consistently asked, "Why has no one ever shown me this before?"

RICHARD BORGONON, chairman of 10ofthose Ltd. and founder of The Word One to One

How to Talk about Jesus

(Without Being **THAT** Guy)

How to Talk about Jesus

(Without Being **THAT** Guy)

PERSONAL EVANGELISM IN A SKEPTICAL WORLD

Sam Chan

ZONDERVAN REFLECTIVE

ZONDERVAN REFLECTIVE

How to Talk about Jesus (Without Being That *Guy)*
Copyright © 2020 by Sam Chan

Requests for information should be addressed to:
Zondervan, *3900 Sparks Dr. SE, Grand Rapids, Michigan 49546*

Zondervan titles may be purchased in bulk for educational, business, fundraising, or sales promotional use. For information, please email SpecialMarkets@Zondervan.com.

ISBN 978-0-310-11269-3 (softcover)

ISBN 978-0-310-11272-3 (audio)

ISBN 978-0-310-11271-6 (ebook)

Cover design: Thinkpen Design
Cover photo: Giamportone / Shutterstock
Interior design: Kait Lamphere

Printed in the United States of America

24 25 26 27 28 LBC 14 13 12 11 10

Contents

Foreword

I believe Jesus' last words should be our first priority.

His last earthly words—between his resurrection and his ascension—were predominantly a commission to us. Those words were a call to tell the good news of the gospel to a hurting world. One of the reasons I came to the Wheaton College Billy Graham Center is that I have a passion for sharing the gospel. I believe we all need a renewed focus on gospel sharing, and I want to be part of that renewal.

There are, however, both challenges and opportunities we face when we think about sharing the gospel in our world today. We face *challenges* in two key categories. The first challenge is **the reputation of the church in society.** There are many people (particularly those who are more secular) who have a general sense that the church is not the solution; in fact, they believe it may be part of the problem. In a world where there is a growing sense of outrage and the rise of cancel culture, churches that believe the gospel should be shared are seen as the problem. Yet the Bible does tell us the gospel is to be shared. We don't have the option to cut and paste to make a Bible of our choosing.

In this third millennium of Christianity, the main way

we've been doing gospel work for the past forty to fifty years has been to invite our friends to church. I remember hearing pastors whom I know, love, and appreciate use words like *invest* and *invite*. So believers were encouraged to invest in others and invite them to a service, while the pastor's job was to share the gospel. In the past, when people had a more positive perception of church, we could do this effectively.

Today, however, we're in an increasingly secular context, as is much of the Western world. Most of what we did for the last four or five decades has been what's called "church evangelism," and that's not a bad thing. But cultural issues, our belief in the uniqueness of Christ, evangelicals' vocal affiliation with politics, questions of morality and sexuality, and more have caused the church to be seen as part of the problem instead of the solution.

The second challenge is **the reputation of individual Christians**. Think of the American version of *The Office* television show, where Angela is the stereotypical Christian character. The actress is a Christian in real life, but her character on the show is hypocritical and judgmental. In one episode, Jim asks several people what three books each would want on a desert island:

Jim: "Angela?"

Angela: "The Bible."

Stanley: "That's one book. You've got two others."

Angela: "*The Purpose Driven Life.*"

Jim: "Nice. Third book?"

Angela: "No."

Her curt reply demonstrated her judgmental attitude toward her questioners. The perception of many unchurched people is that Christians are judgmental and hypocritical in what they believe and say.

But in the face of these challenges, we also have two powerful *opportunities* before us. The first opportunity is **the proximity of witness**. In the coming years, we must have a greater emphasis on personal evangelism. Let me be clear: I'm not against church evangelism. In fact, it is very effective in some places but increasingly rare in others. But I believe a greater focus on personal evangelism may be able to overcome the abstract bias against the broader church and Christians in general. Your neighbor, coworker, or relative may have a broadly negative view of Christians, but because that person knows you, the proximity of witness creates a more positive perception of the message being received.

Second, I believe with all my heart that **evangelism needs to move out of the hands of professionals**. I thank God for both pastors and evangelists, but we have overprofessionalized evangelism to the detriment of mission. The end result is the de-emphasis of each Christian's personal call to fulfill the Great Commission.

Spiritual gift tests became all the rage in the 1970s and 1980s. One of the gifts often listed was the gift of evangelism. Here's the problem: there's no gift of evangelism in the Bible; there's the gift of the *evangelist* we read about in Ephesians 4:11 (ESV): "And he gave the apostles, the prophets, the evangelists, the shepherds and teachers."

But what do the evangelists do? Verse 12 reads, "To equip the saints for the work of ministry." Renewing a focus on the personal call to share leads to the deprofessionalization of evangelism and a broader engagement with the people of God, who then see their role as showing and sharing the love of Jesus.

When we experienced the great shutdown of church services during the Covid-19 pandemic, people said, "Well, what do we do now? We can't invite our friends to church." But here's the amazing thing: even in a time when people won't come to a big group, we can still share the gospel with our neighbor.

It is time to reengage a spirit of personal evangelism in fresh ways in the life of every believer.

My friend Sam Chan believes this as well. You can sense this as you read this timely book. Sam will help you learn how to share Christ in ways that are effective in the situations we find ourselves today and help you move from guilt over not sharing Jesus to confidence in telling others the good news of God.

Sam has taken the best theological and practical ideas from evangelism training in the past and companioned them with timeless missiological principles and effective tools in a postmodern culture. He has been teaching these principles for years to everyone, from college students to urban professionals, and I'm glad he is sharing his wisdom with us here.

Sam is a knowledgeable and experienced witness and teacher. He holds a PhD from Trinity Evangelical Divinity School and has spent years sharing Christ with college students, lawyers, and other professionals in his home city of Sydney, Australia.

Most Christians fail to share Christ regularly for one of two reasons. Either they fear being ostracized for speaking up about Jesus, becoming stigmatized as "*that* guy," or they feel helpless and are afraid to share because they are sure they will fail. You will find both comfort and confidence in this book as it walks you through both the why and the how of our witness today.

I'm not discouraged, in part because of books like this that help God's people intentionally and strategically reengage personal evangelism as a central component of our discipleship. I believe the opportunity for gospel work and witness is great and ongoing before us. And I believe Sam Chan has given the church a gift through this wonderful resource.

Ed Stetzer (PhD), executive director of the
Wheaton College Billy Graham Center and
professor and dean at Wheaton College

Introduction

I boarded my plane in Boston at 10:00 p.m. The plane didn't move. Finally the captain announced there was an electrical problem. Engineers were working hard to fix it, but it meant our plane would sit at the gate for the next few hours—with all of us still buckled into our seats.

I, along with most of my fellow passengers, fell asleep in my seat as we waited to take off. Around 2:00 a.m., an announcement woke me up. "Is there a doctor on the plane?" As a medical doctor, I love it when this happens. Usually it's not a real emergency, just something minor, and afterward the crew thanks you and sometimes gives you a gift.

I frantically pushed the call button and proudly announced, "I'm a doctor!"

I followed a crew member to the plane's galley, where I saw a passenger lying on the floor having a heart attack. This time it was a real emergency.

Fortunately for me, another doctor had gotten there first and was already crouched at the passenger's head. "Well, looks like you won't need me," I said to the crew member. But he urged me to stay, just in case.

What you need to understand is this: As a doctor, there's *nothing* you can do to treat a heart attack when you're stuck on a plane. All you can do is support the patient until the emergency team arrives and evacuates the patient. And if you're stuck at the *feet* of the patient, like I was, there's *absolutely nothing* you can do.

The other doctor seemed to know what he was doing. He asked for a stethoscope and started listening to the patient's heart. Then he asked for a blood pressure cuff and took the patient's blood pressure. Then he asked for the patient's medication bag and gave the patient some heart medication. Then he asked for an oximeter and used it to measure the patient's oxygen saturations. He repeated this process over and over while we waited for the emergency team to show up.

After the emergency team arrived and sped the patient off to the nearest emergency room, I went up to the other doctor and said, "Well done back there. By the way, what sort of doctor are you?"

He looked at me very sheepishly and said, "I'm an allergist."

An allergist! *Well played. Well played*, I thought.

As an orthopedic surgical assistant, I was not much use in a heart attack. But an allergist was even worse equipped than I was. He must have felt even more scared and helpless than I had.

A lot of being a doctor is putting on a brave show when deep down you have no idea what you're doing. You just know that you'd better do something, and it had better look good. And this is exactly what participating in evangelism feels like today. We want to tell our friends about Jesus. We're told that we need to tell our friends about Jesus.

But we don't know how to do it. When it comes to evangelism, we are scared and helpless.

This is a unique time for the Christian church in the West. At one time, humanity lived in a pre-Christian world. This was the time of the Roman Empire, before Christianity existed. Then humanity entered the world of Christendom. This was a time when the Christian church and its leaders were part of the ruling elite. Christianity was represented in government, courts of law, and schools. But now, for the first time ever, we are in a *post*-Christian world.

This is why evangelism is so scary and awkward. The methods of evangelism that worked so well in the past no longer seem effective today. What worked in the age of Christendom seems ineffective in our post-Christian age.

Worse, the culture of our post-Christian age has a negative view of personal evangelism. Our society sees evangelism as offensive, inappropriate, and insensitive.

This leaves us in a difficult dilemma. If we don't tell our friends about Jesus, we feel like we're not doing what Jesus wants us to do. But if we try to tell our friends about Jesus, our efforts feel clunky, awkward, and weird. As a result, we rarely evangelize. We're worried we'll lose our friends or offend our family members. We don't want to become "that uncle" at the Thanksgiving dinner.

My previous book, *Evangelism in a Skeptical World*, promised to "make the unbelievable news of Jesus more believable."[1] It acknowledged the challenge of evangelism in our post-Christian world and suggested some fresh ways of doing evangelism. The book must have scratched an itch because way more people bought it than I expected.

One shortcoming of that book was that it served as a textbook that addressed many of the concerns of *professional* evangelism—evangelism done by those in professional Christian ministry. That's why I'm writing this follow-up book. This book is for everyday Christians, not just those in professional ministry. It focuses on *personal* evangelism. It uses less technical language.[2] This book will repeat some of the material from *Evangelism in a Skeptical World*, but it will offer new material and insights as well.

My goal in this book is to help you tell your friends about Jesus—without being "*that* guy." Hopefully, by the time you finish this book, you will be equipped with fresh insights for personal evangelism. You will be confident and competent in evangelism. You will walk away thinking not just, *I can do that*, but also, *I can't wait to do this!*

Sadly, I can't promise that this book will help if you're dealing with a heart attack on a plane.

God Sends the Fire

But We Still Need to Build the Altar

When it comes to evangelism, I believe that it's God's work. After all, the message of the gospel belongs to God. This is why Paul calls it "the gospel *of God*" (Romans 1:1, emphasis added).

I once heard Timothy Keller compare our work of evangelism with Elijah's work of building the altar at Mount Carmel in 1 Kings 18. Elijah built the altar, but it was God who sent the fire. Elijah couldn't send the fire.

In the same way, when it comes to evangelism, it is God who "sends the fire." God pours out his Spirit. God opens the heart of the person hearing the good news (Acts 16:14). God sovereignly and supernaturally rebirths the person, moving them from darkness to light, from death to life (Ephesians 2:5).

Only God can send the fire. But as Keller points out, *Elijah still had to build the altar*. In the same way, we also have our part to play in evangelism. The gospel belongs to God. But he chooses to use us to tell it in our natural and mundane human words—using our own personal relationships, listening skills, personalities, experiences, stories, emotions, and gospel outlines. This is why Paul also calls it "*my* gospel, the message *I* proclaim about Jesus Christ" (Romans 16:25, emphasis added).

In the following pages, I will share eight personal tips on evangelism. They are my own personal natural, mundane, and human ways of trying to tell my friends the gospel. But they also require the sovereign and supernatural working of God. I pray that God uses these tips to move your friends from death to life.

Merge Your Universes

Evangelism Is a Lifestyle Change

Let me tell you two stories. Here's the first one:

> Last night, my wife and I were kicking back watching TV when a UFO landed in our backyard. A little green man got out and invited us into his UFO. So my wife and I went inside. The UFO took us to Jupiter. We met the little green man's friends and family and had a meal together. Afterward we got back into the UFO and traveled back to planet Earth. And we must have traveled through a time portal, because only one second of earth time had gone by.

Do you believe me? Of course not. Now let me tell you the second story:

> About two thousand years ago, God sent us his son, Jesus. He was born of a virgin. And he was 100 percent God and 100 percent human at the same time. When he walked on earth, he did amazing things—like raise a dead girl back to life, give sight to a man born blind, turn thirty gallons of water into wine, and feed five

1

thousand people with a few loaves and fish. But more than that, he died on a cross. Three days later, he rose from the dead. His Spirit lives in you right now. But more than that, Jesus ascended into heaven—where he is right now! And if you believe this, God will wash away all your sin, guilt, and shame. And when you die, your soul will rise up to be with Jesus in heaven. One day Jesus will come again and set up a physical kingdom here on earth. And when that happens, your body will rise from its grave and be reunited with your soul.

Do you believe me now? To many people, the story about Jesus sounds ridiculously unbelievable (even though it's true). If we're honest, we have to admit that the UFO story may even be more believable than the Jesus story. Yet we believe the Jesus story anyway.

One reason we're hesitant to evangelize is that we're worried our friends may find the Jesus story a little too hard to believe. We know it's true, but how can we convince them it is? What if I told you that your non-Christian friends are more likely to believe the Jesus story than you think?

Plausibility Structures

We are happy to believe the Jesus story over the UFO story because of what sociologists call *plausibility structures*. We all have plausibility structures that determine whether a story is unbelievable or believable. These plausibility structures are essentially preprogrammed and predetermined inside us.

As I was telling you the UFO story, your plausibility structures were flashing red lights and setting off blaring alarms. When I said that this little green man took us to his home planet Jupiter and we went through a time portal and only one second of earth time went by, your plausibility structures were screaming, "Unbelievable!"

But when I told you the Jesus story, your plausibility structures were giving you green lights. When I said that Jesus was born of a virgin and that he died on a cross and rose again three days later, your plausibility structures were saying, "Believable!" And when I said that Jesus will come again, your plausibility structures kept giving you green lights.

Where do these plausibility structures come from? Three main sources contribute to our plausibility structures: (1) community, (2) experiences, and (3) facts, evidence, and data.

Regarding the UFO story, most of you do not belong to a *community*—friends and family you know and trust—that believes in UFOs. Most of you have never had a personal *experience* of a UFO in your life. And most of you do not believe there are any *facts*, *evidence*, or *data* to support my UFO story. That's why you judge the UFO story to be unbelievable.

But regarding the Jesus story, most of you do belong to a *community* that believes in Jesus. Most of you have had a personal *experience* of Jesus in your life. And most of you do believe that there are enough *facts*, *evidence*, and *data* to support the Jesus story. That's why you judge the Jesus story to be believable.

Which is the most powerful source in determining belief? You might assume it's facts, evidence, and data. Maybe you desperately want it to be facts, evidence, and data. But facts, evidence, and data are actually the least powerful in determining belief.

You see, if I told you the UFO is still in my backyard right now, you probably couldn't be bothered to come and check it out. You probably don't have the time or willpower to investigate what is so unbelievable. And if you did bother to check it out, you would find a way to explain away the evidence. You would tell yourself that this was all part of an elaborate hoax.

Facts, evidence, and data are surprisingly weak in making something believable. So which is the most powerful in determining belief? Community.

The Power of Community

The term *community* refers to friends and family we know, love, and trust. Community is the most powerful force in determining belief. Community shapes the way we interpret our experiences. Community shapes the way we interpret facts, evidence, and data.

When I lived in Australia, I played and watched rugby. I was convinced it was the roughest, most brutal sport in the world. After all, rugby players wear no helmets. You can't get much tougher than that! And I believed that American football was the least tough sport in the world. After all, players in the NFL have to wear pads and helmets. You can't get much softer than that! This was my entirely rational belief based on clear evidence and logical proof.

But when I lived in Chicago, my American friends convinced me that American football was way more brutal precisely because football players wear helmets. Have you ever watched a helmet-to-helmet hit? After a while, I believed my American friends.

Why did I change my beliefs? Because I had changed my community from one set of friends to another. I had swapped one set of "plausibility structures" for another. And my new set of plausibility structures made me interpret the *same evidence*—NFL players wear helmets—in a new and different way.

Brexit and the Power of Community

In June 2016, the United Kingdom held a referendum to vote on Brexit—whether to withdraw from the European Union. The vote ended up sharply dividing the UK. Roughly 52 percent voted in favor of Brexit, and 48 percent voted against it.

Analysts believe that those who voted in favor of Brexit mainly had friends who were also in favor of Brexit. And those who voted against Brexit mainly had friends who were also against Brexit. In other words, people voted according to how their group of friends voted.

In the months leading up to the vote, countless debates about Brexit took place in all forms of media. Everyone was exposed to both sides of the debate—they knew the reasons for and against Brexit. But it is estimated that not one person changed their mind on how they were going to vote. Whatever way they were going to vote prior to hearing both sides of the debate is exactly how they voted after hearing the debates. Their group of friends mainly determined how they interpreted the evidence. Their minds were already made up.

Whether we like it or not, whether we know it or not, community determines how we believe. We think like those around us think. We behave like those around us behave. And we believe what those around us believe.

Sometimes the effects of community are subtle. For instance, when we were expecting our second child, my wife, Stephanie, and I spent a lot of time trying to work out what name to give this child. We didn't want to give the child a name that was too common, but we didn't want to give the child a name that was too funky either. We wanted something in that sweet spot in the middle—a name that declares to the world just how trendy and fashionable we are as parents. We decided on the name Cooper. Little did we know that Cooper was one of the top-ten baby names in our state that year. We had picked a common name. We were sheep—just following the pack—even though we didn't realize it.

Our community—whether we are conscious of it or not—determines what we think, how we behave, and what we believe.

The UFO story is unbelievable because I am the one and only bozo who believes it. But imagine that I told you the UFO story in a room full of people, and imagine that after I told it, half the people in the room screamed, "Me too! That also happened to me last night." My UFO story would be much more believable because half the people you know and trust also believe it. If all the people in the room were to say, "Me too! That also happened to me last night," my story would be *highly* believable—and you would feel like a bozo for not believing.

Paul recognized the power of community and belief. In 1 Corinthians 15:5–8, Paul says that after Christ rose from the dead, "he appeared to Cephas, and then to the Twelve. After that, he appeared to more than five hundred of the brothers and sisters at the same time, most of whom are still living . . . Then he appeared to James, then to all the apostles, and last of all he appeared to me also." Paul may seem to be overly thorough here. Not only did he himself see Jesus risen from the dead, but the other apostles also saw Jesus risen from the dead, and so did five hundred other people you can talk to right now. Paul says this because his testimony is way more believable if five hundred other people—people you know, love, and trust—also believe it.

I want to be clear: I'm talking about the *believability* of a story and not how *true* it is. Jesus *is* risen from the dead, whether you choose to believe it or not. But a story, no matter how true, is hard to believe if no one else in your community believes it.

Community and Evangelism

Typically, when we as Christians get fired up to do evangelism, we go out solo. We go and sign up for a book club or a cooking class or a football team, hoping to be the one person who tells them about Jesus.

These solo efforts are admirable and worthy. But the result is that we are the one and only bozo in the room who believes in the Jesus story. And no matter how true this story is, no matter how much evidence we can produce, no matter how logically we argue, our story—as true, logical, and rational as it is—remains unbelievable because there's no other person in the room who also believes it.

One of the major reasons our friends aren't Christians is that they don't belong to a community of friends who also believe in Jesus. It's not primarily because they haven't heard the gospel (they probably haven't, but they already think they know what you believe). It's not because there's not enough evidence for the Christian faith (because no matter how much evidence you produce, they'll explain it away). In many cases, the number one reason our friends aren't Christians is that they don't have any other Christian friends.

So what we need to do is introduce them into a community of Christian friends. How do we do this? By getting our Christian friends to become friends with our non-Christian friends.

The Non-Christian Bubble

I read the *New York Times* every day. It's my number one go-to source for news. I also love its crossword puzzles. But I've heard that many of the staff members at the *New York Times* do not know any Christians. It's not just that they don't have any friends who are Christians; they actually don't know a single real-life Christian!

So it's not just Christians who can live in a bubble. Our non-Christian friends often live in a bubble with only non-Christian contacts.

Merge Our Universes

Typically, as Christians, we have two separate universes of friends. We have a universe of Christian friends, and we have another universe of non-Christian friends. We keep these two universes separate from each other. When our Christian friends go to the movies, we go along with them. When our non-Christian friends have a barbecue, we go along with them.

But what we need to do is *merge our universes*. So when our Christian friends go to the movies, we invite our non-Christian friends along. Or when our non-Christian friends have a barbecue, we bring some of our Christian friends along. Bit by bit, our Christian friends will become friends with our non-Christian friends. We will have merged our universes.

When I was a junior medical doctor, I lived in an apartment with three non-Christian junior medical doctors. Whenever my Christian friends from church came over to hang out with me, they also hung out with my non-Christian doctor friends. When my Christian friends went out to the movies, they also invited my non-Christian doctor friends—and vice versa. After two years, we had merged our universes. (Because that's approximately how long it takes to form a new network of friends—two years.) After two years, all three of my junior doctor friends gave their lives to Christ. They had entered a community of believers.

What I'm arguing for here is a lifestyle change, not a one-off event. We need to proactively and deliberately work at merging our universes. It's a bit like making a New Year's resolution to get in shape. We tell ourselves, "This year. This year. Really. This year, I'm going to get fit." We sign up for a gym. We get up at 5:00 a.m. and go for a run. But this never lasts. It's unsustainable because it's yet another activity that we're trying to shoehorn into our already busy lifestyle. Fitness requires a lifestyle change rather than an extra activity we tack onto our lives.

It's the same with evangelism. It requires a lifestyle change. It's not a one-off event where we try to tell our friends about Jesus. Instead, we need to become evangelistic. Evangelism is more than something we do; it's something we become. And it's the same with our local church. Our church can't just shoehorn extra evangelistic events into its busy schedule. Our church needs to become evangelistic. It's a lifestyle change.

Midlife Crisis Meets Evangelism

Paul was married and had young children. He was successful in his work. He was financially independent. He was secure in his Christian faith. What was his next step? Paul did what any man in his position would do—he bought that loud, fast, expensive car he had been dreaming about ever since he was a little boy.

But that still didn't seem to fill a hole in his life. Perhaps Paul could do more to tell his friends about Jesus. God seemed to have blessed Paul with a lot of non-Christian friends and contacts. So Paul went to the other men in his church. They were also in their midlife, financially successful, and owned nice cars. Together, they formed a car club. Next, they started inviting their non-Christian friends to the club. In just a few weeks, the car club had grown from eight to forty members.

Now a typical Sunday for Paul and his friends looks like this. They meet at 6:00 a.m. and go for a drive on some twisty and hilly roads. Afterward they eat breakfast together at a café. Then, quite abruptly, at 9:00 a.m., half of the group gets up en masse and leaves for their church's morning worship service.

Out of curiosity, many of the non-Christians started to ask if they could go with the Christians to their church. They wanted to check it out. For many of the men, this was a huge change of heart. One man's wife didn't believe her husband was going to a church until she checked the location tracker on his phone.

Making Friends in Today's World

The number of friends we have changes, depending on our stage of life. You know how it works. When you're in elementary school, you have a handful of friends. When you're in high school, you have more friends. When you get to college, you have hundreds and hundreds of friends—so many friends, in fact, that you don't know who *not* to invite to your twenty-first birthday party or wedding. And then after you get married, you have *no friends*. No one wants to hang out with you, and you don't want to hang out with anyone. You just want to stay home. But then you have kids, and your universe of friends takes off again because your kids start making friends, and you begin hanging out with their friends' parents. As we get older still, our universe of friends will start shrinking again, but the nature of friendship will change. We consolidate our friendships. So while we might lose out on quantity of friends, we'll gain in terms of quality of friendships.[3]

Somehow, in the last few years, my wife, Steph, and I have found our universe of non-Christian friends to be expanding rapidly. These friends are far wiser, wittier, and more interesting than my wife and I could ever be. They bring us joy, goodness, and karaoke nights.

Steph and I have noticed that the majority of our non-Christians friends have moved into our city in the last few years. They haven't had time to establish a network of friends yet. So it's been really easy for us to move into their world and become part of their network of trusted friends.

These days, people are frequently moving—changing houses, schools, and jobs. They are moving into new neighborhoods and don't have a network of friends. And it's going to be really hard for them to make any friends.

Sociologists say that human beings need friendships at three different levels. First, they need a tribe of 150 people for belonging, status, and identity. Second, they need a network of thirty friends. And third, they need an inner circle of five trusted friends—the sort of friends you can call on for a favor, to help you move to a new house, or to babysit your kids in an emergency. Studies are now showing that most people in the West lack this tribe, network, and inner circle.[4] That's why we'll drive twenty minutes to the store for milk instead of asking our next-door neighbor for it.

It's harder now than ever before to make friends because of our fractured, isolated, and transient lifestyles.[5] Studies show that loneliness is the new health epidemic in the West.[6] Sixty percent of Australians report themselves as lonely, and 80 percent say it's a problem in their world.[7] As a result, though, that means it's easier than ever for Christians to make friends with non-Christians. They don't have a tribe. They don't have a network. They don't have an inner circle. So it should be really easy for us to present ourselves as the trusted tribe, network, and friends they need.

Here are a couple ways to build up your circle of non-Christian friends.

How to Be a Neighbor

One way to make friends is simply to get to know your neighbors. For a while, my wife and I were renting. We moved frequently. Over time, we developed a simple routine that we still use whenever we move into a new house.

First, we visit all our immediate neighbors—usually the two houses on our right, the two houses on our left, and the four houses opposite us. We give them a simple gift—fruit, nuts, beer, or wine—and a card with our names and phone numbers. And then we ask for their names—and write them down before we forget.

Next we knock on their doors around Christmas and Easter and give them a simple card and gift. Bit by bit, we get to know them more. We invite them over for meals or do double-date nights with them. Often when we bake, we share the extra cookies or cakes we've made.

We also ask our neighbors for favors because we've found that, perhaps counterintuitively, you can build more relational trust by *asking* for a favor. By asking for a favor, we make ourselves vulnerable. We have placed ourselves in their debt. It's a funny way to earn trust, but it works. And slowly we found that our neighbors were happy to ask favors from us in return.

Through this strategy, we eventually become the village hub. We become the social glue that holds the street together. As our neighbors begin to exchange Christmas gifts and goodies and invite each other to birthday parties, we slowly but surely form a community.

But more than that, we have a street where non-Christian neighbors are becoming friends with Christian neighbors. It's a merged universe of friends.

Matchmake Your Friends

When I was single, people were always trying to matchmake me. They'd invite me to a party, and I would turn up, naively thinking it was just a party. But it soon became obvious what was happening. There's a couple, another couple, and yet another couple—and then there's a single girl all by herself. And look, they've even placed us together at the dinner table. How did I not see this coming?

But now my wife and I do the same thing. Except we're not trying to matchmake a guy with a girl romantically; we're trying to matchmake our non-Christian friends with our Christian friends socially.

It's simple. We put on a social event, like a barbecue or a Super Bowl party, and invite some non-Christian friends. And then we think of Christian friends who have something in common with our non-Christian friends. We throw them together and watch them become friends with each other. We've found that a good ratio is 1:2—that is, for every non-Christian friend, we invite two Christian friends. That way, our non-Christian friends will find it easier to adopt the Christians' plausibility structures.

Is This Friendship Evangelism in Disguise?

An American friend once dismissed this whole approach to evangelism as "friendship evangelism." That's when I realized I was a naive Australian who had unknowingly stumbled into an American minefield—one that distinguishes "friendship" evangelism from "proclamation" evangelism. The theory of "friendship" evangelism is to make friends with non-Christians, with the hope of one day telling them about Jesus. I'm okay with this. But the criticism from some circles is that, in practice, this day never arrives. The theory of "proclamation" evangelism is that the essence of evangelism is to tell someone the gospel. Until that happens, we have not truly evangelized. I'm also okay with this. But the criticism from some circles is that, in practice, this is way harder than it sounds. It's easy to do with strangers, but not with friends. So this day also never arrives.

To be clear, I'm not suggesting we just make friends and never tell them about Jesus. I'm suggesting that unless we make friends, we have no one to tell about Jesus. Even better, I'm suggesting we do *friends* (plural) evangelism, where *many* Christian friends—not just me—are telling my non-Christian friends about Jesus. My friends will be more likely to believe precisely because they now have many Christian friends who also believe in Jesus.

The Gospel Isn't a Tribal Badge Marker

One of the flip sides to the power of community is that certain beliefs can become "tribal badge markers."

Let's say I'm an Oakland Raiders fan. I might wear a Raiders jersey as a "tribal badge marker." This identifies me as a card-carrying, loyal Raiders fan. It signals to other Raiders fans that we are of the same tribe. In return, I will receive affirmation, belonging, status, security, and lots of high fives from other members of my tribe.

Unfortunately, as we become more and more polarized in our culture wars, certain beliefs also function as tribal badge markers. Your tribe—red or blue, left or right, progressive or conservative—will adopt certain stances on immigration, law and order, health, education, environment, and guns that are essentially tribal badge markers. It's no longer only about the facts, evidence, or truth; it's about what your tribe believes.

Thus, if you choose an alternative belief on, let's say, immigration, this is like swapping your Raiders jersey for a Broncos jersey. Your original tribe will shame, expel, or punish you.[8] You will feel you no longer belong. You will change tribes. But what usually happens is the opposite. You will never change your views on immigration, no matter what evidence you're presented with, simply so you can be loyal to your tribe.

For evangelism, this means at least two things. First, we should try to avoid playing the "culture wars" game. The gospel should not be a tribal badge marker for one side against another side. We should not make it an "us versus them" thing.[9] If it becomes that, our friend will refuse to believe the gospel because it will mean they are disloyal to their tribe. They will double down on their nonbelief.[10]

Evangelism should be a process in which we point to our shared common humanity, one in which we share enough humility to admit that we are all broken, no matter which tribe we belong to. And one in which we share a

common human need for Jesus to rescue us.[11] The gospel of
Jesus Christ should transcend every culture war.

If we merge our universes and get our Christian friends
to become friends with our non-Christian friends, then we
become members of the same tribe. The gospel will become
one of many things that our tribe can happily believe.

They Came On Church Buses

People often ask me, "Why can't we just evangelize the
same way Billy Graham did?" What's wrong with a
simple twenty-minute Bible talk? The hidden assumption
here is that if it worked for Billy, it should work for us.
Perhaps there's also the feeling that we're selling out on
the gospel by not trusting the power of a twenty-minute
Bible talk.

I'm old enough to have been at several of Billy Graham's
talks in 1979. I experienced it all—the twenty-minute Bible
talk, the prayer of response, the choir singing "Just as I Am"
as Billy made the appeal for people to come to the front.
Billy even said his famous signature statement: "Come
down . . . the buses will wait."

The buses will wait.

What does that mean? It means that the non-Christians
who came that night came on a *church bus*. If you were
a non-Christian at a Billy Graham talk that night, you
didn't walk in off the street; you came on a church bus.

You came with a *community of believers*. Two-thirds of the people on that bus with you were believers. You adopted the plausibility structures of the believers on the church bus. So when Billy gave his Bible talk, the good news of Jesus was *believable*.

Rico Tice, a gifted UK evangelist, talks about three cultural phases of evangelism in the West. The first phase was in the late twentieth century, the time when Billy Graham was giving his talks. His audience was *Christianized*. Even though they weren't believers, they had Christian friends and had grown up in Sunday school. Billy's talk only had to be twenty minutes because he was asking them to believe what they already knew to be true.

The second phase was in the early twenty-first century. Here the audience sort of knew the gospel. But they also had "defeater beliefs" that stopped them from believing this gospel. For instance, what about other religions? What about science? What about evil? Here our job was to remove these defeater beliefs and clear the way for them to believe the gospel.

The third phase of evangelism is where we are now. Today, our audience is in a completely different universe. They don't know of the gospel. They don't even know why they should care. It's of no relevance to them. And deep down, they suspect that the gospel is a tool of oppression used by those who used to be in power. They are hermetically shut off from the good news of Jesus.

This is why we need to merge our universes. It's one of the most powerful ways our friends can come into contact with the gospel.

Flipping the Sequence

It used to be that when Billy Graham came and preached about Jesus, people heard the gospel and *believed*. Then they would be plugged into a church to find *belonging*. When they joined the church, they received instruction from the Bible on how to *behave*. The sequence was BELIEF → BELONGING → BEHAVIOR.

Now that we are in a post-Christian age, the sequence seems to go the other way. People first find *belonging* with Christians. They make friends with our Christian friends. They play soccer with us on our church team. They come to the playgroup that meets in our church building. Soon they start *behaving* the same way we do. They sign up for our rosters. They volunteer with us. They join one of our small groups to start reading the Bible. Eventually this leads to *belief* in Jesus. The sequence now seems to be BELONGING → BEHAVIOR → BELIEF.

We can look for ways to help our non-Christian friends find *belonging* with us. Then we can try to *do things* with them. By doing things together, they might see things from our point of view and gradually also want to *share our belief*.

Evangelism Is a Team Game

Nathan Campbell, an Australian pastor and blogger, came up with the phrase, "Evangelism in a skeptical world is basically a *team game*."[12] We need to do evangelism together, as a team, playing off the same playbook.

Nathan showed me that in 1 Thessalonians 1:4–10, which is one of the great go-to passages for a model of Paul's evangelism, Paul writes, "You know how *we* lived among you" (v. 5, emphasis added). For way too long I had misread that verse as, "You know how *I* lived among you." But Paul says *we*.

It was a *community* of believers who lived among the pre-believing Thessalonians. Not just Paul the individual. It was a community. In other words, evangelism is more than me going out solo to tell my friends about Jesus. My community of Christian friends also needs to *live among* my non-Christian friends and become their friends.

We can introduce our Christian friends to our non-Christian friends. We can become their tribe, village, and community. And then, bit by bit, the story of Jesus will be more believable than they had ever dared to imagine.

Go to Their Things

And They Will Come to Your Things

It was the Friday night before the Australia Day (which is Australia's equivalent to the USA's July 4th) weekend holiday. My wife, Steph, and I were inside an old-school bar where the walls, floor, and ceiling were painted black—because, quite simply, it's easier to clean up the mess afterward if the surfaces are black. The place was packed. Standing room only. We were squeezed in shoulder to shoulder with two hundred other people.

The band on the stage was playing rock-and-roll anthems. These were the sort of anthems where the whole crowd sings along because everyone knows the words. Think of songs like Journey's "Don't Stop Believin'" or Bon Jovi's "Livin' on a Prayer." The only difference was that all the anthems were Aussie anthems in homage to the Australia Day weekend holiday.

The band was good. They mixed up power ballads with upbeat anthems. They worked the crowd into a happy frenzy. Everyone knew the words. Everyone was singing. Everyone was having a good time.

When it was all over, the lights went off and the band walked off the stage. The crowd was cheering. And then, in the darkness, the crowd started chanting, "One more song! One more song! One more song!"

The lights came back on. The band walked back onto the stage. The crowd roared.

Can you guess what song the band played as the final *encore* song for the night? Think about it. If you're the band, this is going to be the climactic song that ushers in the Australia Day weekend holiday. In effect, you are choosing the unofficial Australian national anthem. But at the same time, it's got to be an upbeat song that the crowd knows the words to and can sing along to.

The band struck the first chord, and the crowd recognized the song instantly. They roared with delight. And I stood back and watched as two hundred Aussies danced, throbbed, hooted, hollered, and clapped as they sang along to the words, "I'm on the hiiiiiiiiiiiiiiighway to hell!"

On the one hand, this was fitting. AC/DC's "Highway to Hell" may as well be the unofficial Australian anthem. It perfectly represents the Australian larrikin spirit. It's the underdog sticking it to the man. Australia began as a prison colony—its people were sent to Australia by the Brits to die. So this song represents gallows humor: we're going to die, but we may as well have a laugh about it on the way.

Yet on the other hand, I saw (like Jesus did in Matthew 9:37) a field ripe for harvest. Instead of viewing this as a threat to the gospel (you can't get more seemingly opposed to the gospel than a crowd celebrating the fact that they're going to hell), I saw it as an *opportunity* for the gospel. I saw that this is the time for the Christian church to shine. It's our time for strength and not weakness.

As Mark Sayers forecasts in his excellent podcast *This Cultural Moment* (www.thisculturalmoment.com), the tide of secularism has gone so far out that the sheer momentum of the gospel is going to come rushing back in.

But how can we harness this momentum of the gospel? How can we turn this cultural moment into opportunities for the gospel? How can we shine our light? How on earth can we get our friends to let us tell them about Jesus if they're in a bar singing, "I'm on the highway to hell"?

Why Would Anyone Want to Hear the Gospel?

I often get asked to speak at evangelistic events. But I notice that most Christians struggle to bring any friends along to these events. The exception is my friend Andrew. He often organizes evangelistic events like these. And I've noticed that, at each event, Andrew is surrounded by four or five non-Christian friends he's brought along. They're different non-Christian friends each time too. And I've noticed that these friends are happy to be there. I can tell by their body language and smiles as they listen to me talk. I can tell by the way they come up to me afterward to thank me.

So I asked Andrew's wife what their secret was. "How come every time I speak at one of these things, you guys are surrounded by non-Christian friends who are happy to be here?"

She replied, "It's easy. We're always hanging out— dinners, movies, barbecues. We're always going to their things, so they're happy to come to one of our things."

I thought, *That's it! That's the secret! If we go to their things, they will come to our things.*

Think about what normally happens. Your church will put on an evangelistic event, like a men's breakfast. And then they will lay the guilt on the men in the church: "Men! Invite your friends to the evangelistic men's breakfast this Saturday."

So now you're thinking, *Okay. Be brave. Big breaths. I've got to invite one of my friends to this evangelistic men's breakfast.*

And your non-Christian friends are thinking the same thing: *Oh no. Here he comes. You know what he's going to do? He's going to invite us to one of those church things.*

Think about it. Since when do men do breakfast together anyway? And now it's a church—*evangelistic*—thing! With a Bible talk? Why would your friends want to come to one of these?

But if you're going to their things, they will come to your things. If you hang out together normally, then this is just one of many things that you would be doing together. Suddenly, it's not as weird or awkward to invite your friends to one of your things—even if it's a church thing.

The Example of Jesus

In Luke 7, we read the powerful story of a woman anointing and washing Jesus' feet with her hair, tears, and perfume. This scene is so moving that many of us gloss over a key detail: Simon the Pharisee invited Jesus to his home for dinner, and Jesus *went*. Similarly, in Luke 14:1, Jesus *went* to the house of a prominent Pharisee.

Think about it. Jesus was invited to his religious opponents' dinner parties. It was hardly going to be a fun, relaxing social time. The small talk would have been miserable. Yet Jesus went anyway. In other words, Jesus would *go to their things*.

Jesus also went to the dinner parties of those on the opposite end of the religious spectrum—the tax collectors and sinners (e.g., Luke 5:29; 19:5–6). In fact, he did this so much that he got criticized for it. People called him "a glutton and a drunkard" (Luke 7:34) because he was doing too much eating and drinking with unclean people.

What we can learn from Jesus is this: if a non-Christian invites us to one of their things—party, fundraiser, gig—we should make it a top priority to go. I often hear Christians lamenting that they have no non-Christian friends. One way to change this is to make a point of going to whatever meals, parties, or events they invite us to.

Go to Their Things

My wife and I have made it a priority to simply *go*. Birthday parties, children's concerts, school plays, Tupperware parties, fundraisers, barbecues, trivia nights—we will be there. By going to our friends' things, we earn enough trust and relational capital that our friends will happily come to one of our things.

You're probably wondering why my wife and I were in a bar singing Aussie anthems anyway. We were the only two Asians there that night! Well, we were there because our neighbor was playing in the band that night. We were going to one of his gigs to support him and have a great date night out.

One night, a small group from my street was going to the local Catholic church for the Christmas Eve midnight Mass. I asked if I could come along. "Sure!" they said. And I shared a ride with them. After the Mass, on the way home, my neighbors asked what I usually do for Christmas. I replied, "Funny you should ask! I'm the guy who gives the Christmas talk at my local Chinese church. *Would you like to come?*" And they all said yes. So for the next few years, my non-Asian neighbors happily came to my Chinese church for Christmas. They came because I had gone to one of their things first.

Get Onto Their Rosters

I signed up my children for weekend sports, thinking it would be a brilliant way to outsource my parenting. I could simply drop off my kids at practice on Wednesday nights and for the game on Saturdays, while I disappeared and had coffee and read a newspaper by myself.

Unfortunately, a lot has changed in children's sports since I was a child. Now they expect the parents to get involved. You can't just drop off your kid. They want you on the barbecue roster, the umpiring roster, and the running-the-water-on-the-sidelines roster. It's a vortex. It tries to suck you in. Before you know it, you lose your weekends and your life.

I was complaining about this to Russell, my coworker at City Bible Forum. Russell himself recently navigated the whole weekend sports chaos with his son. He told me, "It's like an undertow. Don't fight it. Embrace it. And let it take you." He told me to sign up, get involved, and take an interest. "Before you know it, you become like an unofficial chaplain on the sideline. People will come up to you and share about their struggles in life. They will ask for your advice. And that's when you can tell them about the difference Jesus can make in their life," he said.

So, thanks to Russell, I've repented. I've now signed up *both* my wife and myself for the barbecue roster, the umpiring roster, and the running-the-water-on-the-sidelines roster! What once seemed like an inconvenient commitment has turned into welcome opportunities to share the gospel.

Become Part of Their Village

Once upon a time, when I was a child, a parent simply dropped a child off at school, and that was that. But now schools are becoming the village hub. Our local elementary school runs fairs, movie nights, trivia nights, fundraisers, book parades, memorial services, art shows, and discos.

I believe that in the previous age of Christendom, the church functioned as the village hub. But now that we are in a post-Christian time, the local school has filled the void left by the church.

We can treat this the same way we treat an undertow: *Don't fight it. Embrace it.* When my wife first signed up for our school's PTA, I was horrified. I knew she would be tied up in meeting after meeting. But now I can see the benefits. She has not only earned massive trust and social capital, but she has become part of the village hub. For many members of the PTA, my wife is the *only* Christian person they have ever met or known.

One immediate payoff was that my wife got to organize the school's Christmas concert. Our school usually keeps this concert as secular as possible out of respect for parents and students of other faiths and traditions. I get it. Because we are no longer in Christendom, we can't expect Christianity to be the dominant voice anymore. I don't want to turn this into a culture wars thing. I understand the need for many voices in the public sphere. But wouldn't it be nice if Christians were one of those voices?

Because my wife gets along with everyone in the PTA, she was given enormous freedom to organize the concert. It also helped that she was the vocalist in the band, and all the other band members were Christians—evangelism is a team sport, after all. The end result was that my wife was able to create her own carols playlist—a sensitive mix of both secular and Christian songs—where the audience clearly sang about the wonderful birth of Jesus at the Christmas concert.

This was only possible because she was part of the village.

Where Do I Draw the Line?

People often ask me, "Is there a limit to what we should go to as Christians?" I usually reply with a nuanced answer.

People criticized Jesus for associating so frequently with sinners. When Jesus invited himself over to stay with Zacchaeus, the onlookers gasped in horror: "He has gone to be the guest of a sinner" (Luke 19:7). Similarly, when Jesus went to Levi's party, the religious leaders complained, "Why do you eat and drink with tax collectors and sinners?" (Luke 5:30). In other words, people thought Jesus was morally compromised because he went to these dinners and parties.

We can learn from Jesus' answer to the religious leaders: "It is not the healthy who need a doctor, but the sick. I have not come to call the righteous, but sinners to repentance" (Luke 5:31–32). By calling Levi and his friends "sinners," Jesus is showing that he does not approve of their lifestyle. Jesus is showing that it's possible to associate with sinners without approving of their lifestyle. Association and approval are not the same thing. And Jesus is also saying that it's precisely *because* Levi and his friends are sinners that it's a priority to eat and drink with them.

Yet we must also keep in mind that we are not Jesus. We are not the Son of God. It's so nice that Jesus touches lepers, but if we did that, we could catch leprosy. It's lovely that Jesus holds the hand of a dead girl, but if we did that, we could catch her disease and also die. There are many things Jesus did that we can't copy 100 percent. Similarly, if we associate with "tax collectors and sinners," sooner or later we may find that our moral compass is affected. That's why it's good to let our church pastor know where we're going and why we're doing this—to keep ourselves accountable.

We can also ask how other people will understand our actions. For instance, some Chinese Christians face the dilemma of whether to attend their parents' funerals. Do they go, knowing the funeral may include idol worship? Or do they stay home, knowing they will be failing to honor their parents?

I'm guided by my pastor friend Rohan. He told me that when he was baptized, his gay, atheist uncle turned up at the church to witness it. No one interpreted the uncle's act of showing up as his giving up his atheism and adopting Rohan's Christian faith. Instead, they saw him as an uncle showing honor and respect to his nephew, without adopting his nephew's faith.

Thus it's important to define why we go to the things we do. We are there to honor and respect our friends' birthdays, concerts, and fundraisers. We are there because we are their friends. We are following the example of Jesus.

Just Another Thing to Do Together

Our church designated a particular Sunday as a "Family Service." The whole morning worship service was kid-friendly. Kids were to sit in the front third of the worship center with their parents. Much of the emceeing, Bible reading, prayer, and worship was led by children. Children were provided with musical instruments so they could make lots of loud noise during worship. Instead of the normal sermon, there was a puppet show.

This church service was also deliberately designed for us to invite non-Christian friends to. The puppet show had just as much for the adults as it did for the children—much like a movie like *Shrek* does. If your friends showed up, they enjoyed a fun, relaxed, kid-friendly worship service where the good news of Jesus was clearly, creatively, and sensitively communicated.

There was only one problem. Our service is at 9:00 a.m. In my experience, most of my friends *cannot* attend something at 9:00 a.m. on a Sunday. They've been up late the previous night. This is their chance to sleep in. No one goes to a church service at 9:00 a.m. unless they really have to. Worse, it was a *Chinese* church service, and our friends were not Chinese.

Very optimistically, my wife and I invited about five families to come. At 8:50 a.m., I nervously looked at my watch, wondering whether they would show up. *What was I thinking when I invited them?*

But one by one, the families we had invited showed up. They had a great time. They enjoyed the service. And I could tell that the parents, as well as the children, heard the gospel clearly. Afterward, we talked for a long time outside on the church lawn while having morning tea.

I still struggled to understand why they had bothered to come. (Did I mention the service was at 9:00 a.m.?) But as I looked around, I saw one mother whose birthday party we'd attended. Another family came from our son's weekend football team, where my wife was on the barbecue roster and I had been on the running-the-water-on-the-sidelines roster. Another family came from my son's school, where my wife was involved with the PTA.

Suddenly it dawned on me. We were always going to their things, so they were happy to come to one of our things. We hang out normally. We're part of their village. This would be one of many things we would be doing together anyway. Today, it just happened to be a Sunday worship service at 9:00 a.m. at a Chinese church.

Coffee, Dinner, Gospel

Find Creative Ways to Do Hospitality

We've just finished dinner, and all I want to do is to turn on the TV and chill. But there's a huge mountain of dirty dishes in the sink. The pile is so big. The task is too monumental. It's simply too overwhelming. I don't know where to begin.

That's when my wife, Steph, steps in. She tells me to relax and break it down into concrete, bite-sized, achievable steps. "Here," she tells me, "begin with a fork. Now here's a glass." And bit by bit, the dishes are done. All I had to do was break down a large, complex task into concrete, bite-sized, achievable steps.

It's the same with evangelism. The task of telling our friends about Jesus seems too big. It's too important, too monumental, too overwhelming. Where do we even begin? Relax! We can break it down into three concrete, bite-sized, achievable steps. Here they are:

COFFEE → DINNER → GOSPEL

The Progression of Conversation

To understand why the above steps—*coffee, dinner, gospel*—work so well, we need to understand that there are three layers to a conversation:[13]

INTERESTS → VALUES → WORLDVIEW

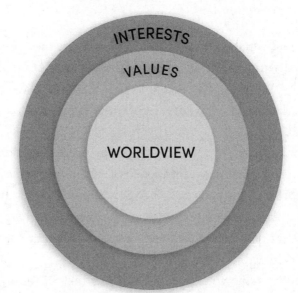

Coffee: The *Interests* Layer

Everything begins with coffee—including evangelism. Coffee is a safe invitation. It's easy to say yes to. It's an investment of ten to twenty minutes. You and your friend will be in a public space.

Your conversation at this coffee stage will usually stay within the first layer of *interests*. Here we talk about things like the weather, what we did on the weekend, and what we're watching on TV. In this layer, the statements will be *descriptive*. They merely describe factual statements that are, by and large, easy to verify. For example, I won't disagree with you when you tell me that the sky is blue; you had a picnic on the weekend; and you're watching K-drama on TV. This is a safe layer for conversations. The talk will be civil. There will be little chance of disagreement.

Many of us are afraid of so-called "small talk" that typically defines the conversation at this stage. But we don't need to be. Small talk is merely talk that's in this *interests* layer of conversation. It sounds superficial, but it functions as a safe area for conversation that won't lead to disagreements or conflict. And if we are good at listening and earn enough trust while talking about interests, eventually we'll be ready to move the conversation to the next layer.

Dinner: The *Values* Layer

After you've done coffee a few times, invite your friend for a meal. This is a bigger invitation, because now you're looking at a time investment of potentially one to two hours. You and your friend will be in more of a private space.

Conversation is now entering the world of *value* statements. In this layer, we make statements about preferences, ethics, values, and beauty. Here we make statements like, "chocolate is better than vanilla," "James Bond movies are better than rom-coms," and "football is better than hockey." On a more serious note, we might talk about where we're going to send our kids to school, who we're going to vote for, and why American cars are better than Japanese cars. The statements in this layer are *prescriptive*. They have a sense of oughtness. They make claims that are, by and large, difficult to verify immediately. As a result, there will be a high chance of disagreement. You may want to take the opposite side of the argument!

While many of us are uncomfortable with small talk, we are even more uncomfortable with conversations that go beyond small talk. It's not because we lack courage or opportunities; it's because, in general, these conversations can end badly. There will be conflicting views. And there are friendships at stake.

But this is the art of conversation. If we show it is safe for them to express themselves and be vulnerable and that we're listening empathetically, we are preparing the way for the next layer of the conversation—where conversations about the gospel can take place.

How do you know when you've reached this point? A friend of mine who was training as a hospital chaplain told me that people will often drop hints that they're ready to move the conversation to the next layer. Our job is to listen intently, pick up on the cues, and simply ask questions like, "Tell me about that," or "How did that make you feel?" That will give them permission to move us into a deeper conversation.

Gospel: The *Worldviews* Layer

At this point, we can try to enter the third layer of conversations, where we start talking about *worldviews*. Here we make statements about what we believe. What is real? What's wrong with the world? Is there a God? Do we pray? Is there life after death? Are humans essentially good or evil? This is the "gospel" step of evangelism because it is in this layer that conversations will naturally, and organically, present us with opportunities to talk about Jesus.

In this layer, our statements will be the *frameworks* for how we view all of the world around us. This is because our worldviews are the engine room that generates and drives our values. Our worldviews shape how we understand facts, evidence, and data. Our worldviews determine how we interpret our personal experiences.

Conversation here can be especially tricky. Our friend may believe in reincarnation. Or that there's no such thing as good and evil. Or that there is no God. In this final layer of conversation, if our friend has a different worldview from ours, we don't just disagree; we actually *disconnect*. We are sitting on two different mountaintops with two different ways of understanding reality, two different ways of interpreting the same evidence.

Moving through the Layers

Typically, as we engage in conversation, we'll naturally progress through the interests and values layers to reach the final worldviews layer. If we earn enough trust in the interests layer, we'll be allowed to progress to the values layer. If we navigate the values layer well, we can look for opportunities to progress to the worldviews layer. There, gradually and organically, gospel conversations will occur. The key to navigating the layers is this: pay attention.

At dinner one time, my friend dropped into the conversation the news that his mother had died earlier that year. I missed the hint. Later that night, he again mentioned that his mother had died. I again missed the hint.

Before the evening was over, he mentioned it a third time. And I missed the hint a third time. On the way home, my wife said, "Do you think he wanted to talk about his mother dying?" I felt like a doofus. All I had to say was something like, "How do you feel about that?" and take his invitation to the next layer of conversation.

Like my friend, people will often offer hints that they're ready to progress deeper. But if our friend isn't giving out any clues, we also have the option of moving the conversation to the next layer ourselves. We do this simply by asking questions. For example, if we ask them what they did on the weekend and they say they played basketball, we can follow up with a values-based question like, "Why do you play basketball on the weekends?" They may respond, "It keeps me healthy." Then we can ask a worldviews-based question like, "Why do we value health so much?"

If we want to expedite the process, we can simply move straight to worldviews. In the same way that questions such as "What did you do on the weekend?" immediately lead to the *interests* layer of conversations, other questions will immediately lead to the *worldviews* layer of conversations. For example, try these questions: "Do you have a faith?" "What religion did your parents raise you with?"[14] or "Do you pray?" I've found that these questions are safe ones to ask because, on the surface, they are still *descriptive*. We're merely asking a factual question. But they also invite the person to share with us their worldview—in particular, their views on the spiritual and the sacred. Sometimes the person will show that they simply don't want to talk about this, and that's okay. We offered them a chance, but they didn't want to open up to us yet. On many other occasions, I've found that people welcome the opportunity to talk about the things that are deepest and most valuable to them.

The Power of Questions

For eight years, I've been the speaker at a CRU (crucamps. com.au) ski camp for teenagers.[15] Every year, my knees tell me I'm too old to be skiing, but I keep coming back because I end up having the most amazing conversations with teens about Jesus.

But how do you get a non-Christian teen to talk about Jesus? One of the camp leaders, Stephanie, asks certain questions when she talks to campers one-on-one. First she'll ask them, "What are you hoping for in life?" or "Where do you want to be in five to ten years' time?"

Sometimes the camper will say "I don't know" or laugh off the question. And that's okay—it simply means they're not ready to make themselves vulnerable by revealing their deeper, true selves to her.

But other campers will give thoughtful responses that reveal their dreams, hopes, goals, and ambitions. With these campers, Stephanie can follow up with, "Why is that important to you?" This invites the camper to explain what is at the core of his or her life: experiences, escape, success, financial security.

Then Stephanie follows up with another question: "What will you do if that doesn't happen?" To answer this, the camper will reveal what is deepest and most important to them. Who are they really? What are they looking for? What is most real to them? What are they most afraid of? What is the one thing in this life they must have?

Stephanie is now in a great position to introduce religion into the conversation.

The type of questions Stephanie asks are what I call "nudge" questions. The nudge question *nudges* the conversation into the next layer. From *interests* to *values*. From *values* to *worldviews*. And from there we nudge the conversation from secular conversation to sacred conversation.

Nudge Questions Act Like a Catalyst

It's also helpful to think of these types of questions as catalyst questions. They act the same way a catalyst acts in chemistry: all the ingredients are there for a chemical reaction, but nothing happens until we add a catalyst. When it comes to evangelism, sometimes all the ingredients are there for a good conversation about Jesus—trust, relationships, friends, hospitality—but we need a nudge question, a catalyst question, to launch the conversation into the next layer.

Nudge questions are designed to give our friend permission to talk about their faith, spirituality, and religion. Here are some examples of nudge questions:

- What are you looking for in life?
- Why is this important to you?

- What is the one thing you absolutely must have in this life?
- What happens if you don't find what you're looking for?
- What do you think it all means?
- What do you believe about God?
- What do you think God wants from you?
- Do you have a faith?
- What religion did your parents raise you with?[16]
- Do you pray?
- What's the *best* thing about being a Muslim?[17]
- Tell me about some traditions, festivals, or celebrations that are important to you?
- What do people get wrong about Islam?

When we ask these questions, the goal is to *listen* and give them the permission to keep on talking. We're not trying to give them advice. We're not trying to have an argument. We're not trying to reason them into the faith. We're not trying to debate them. We're not asking them to defend their position. We are simply using the questions to give them our permission to take the conversation to the next level. It's an invitation, not an inquisition or interrogation.

The Secret Sauce of Evangelism

As an Asian kid, when I was growing up, I never noticed roof racks on cars. That's because Asian parents aren't big on roof racks. They have no need to own roof racks because they don't go surfing or camping. The whole reason your Asian parents make you study so hard is so that you can earn a degree and get a job so you can afford to stay in a hotel and not sleep in a tent for your vacations.

But once I took up surfing and found myself in need of a roof rack, I realized that roof racks are *everywhere*. Why hadn't I noticed them before? Because I wasn't looking for them.

It's the same with hospitality. It's everywhere in the Bible. But for a long time, I was so focused on the "word gifts" in the New Testament like preaching, teaching, and evangelism that I failed to notice how often the idea of hospitality appears in the New Testament.

Almost every New Testament writer uses the word *hospitality*—Acts, Romans, 1 Timothy, Hebrews, 1 Peter, and 3 John. But the *idea* of hospitality goes far beyond this. It's there when Zacchaeus joyfully welcomes Jesus into his home (Luke 19:5–6). It's there when Levi throws a banquet for Jesus and invites his tax-collecting friends (Luke 5:29). It's there when Lydia invites Paul and his companions to her home (Acts 16:15). It's there when the jailer takes Paul and Silas to his home for a meal (Acts 16:34). Interestingly, in many of these examples, it's the nonbeliever who shows hospitality to the believer.

But what's the big deal about hospitality? The three simple steps of evangelism—*coffee, dinner, gospel*—are actually hospitality in disguise. Hospitality provides the space and permission for gospel conversations to occur.

In almost every other area of life, it's difficult to have a conversation deeper than small talk. Sometimes deep conversations are inconvenient—your friend has a bus to catch. Sometimes deep conversations are inappropriate—your friend should be working and not talking to you. Sometimes deep conversations go against social etiquette—it's not the time or place to talk about religion. But the whole point of eating together is providing a space to talk together. Eating together isn't about the food; it's about connecting, relating, and *talking*.

Hospitality is the secret hidden sauce of evangelism. Right now, my wife and I are juggling a multitude of different universes of non-Christian friends. We have the *after-school-swimming-lessons* friends. We have the *weekend-football* friends. And then we have the *playgroup* friends.

So far, the *after-school-swimming-lessons* universe has not been fruitful. We're meeting in a loud, public space, and all the parents rush off straight after the lesson. Similarly, the *weekend-football* universe was not fruitful until we started to have people over for barbecues and introduced them to our Christian friends.

But by far our most fruitful universe has been the *playgroup* universe at our local church. At 10:00 a.m., the parents drop their children off at the playgroup at one end of the church fellowship hall. Then they sit down at the opposite end of the room to have coffee and enjoy small talk for an hour. Because an hour of adult conversation is not enough, my wife then invites the parents to our house for lunch. Now that they're engaging in adult conversation in the privacy of our home, the conversations drift toward values. People linger. Often when I get home from work, the parents are still there. It would be rude to ask them to leave, so my wife invites them to stay for dinner. Conversations drift toward worldviews, and gospel conversations begin.

Many of the non-Christian parents in our playgroup have become friends with the Christian parents. They have checked out their churches, read the Bible with them, and explored Christianity deeper. A significant proportion have become believers. And it all came down to hospitality.

Look for Creative Ways to Do Hospitality

I live on a street where the men have a habit of watering the front lawn by hand with a garden hose. I'm sure their wives are asking, "Why can't you use a sprinkler?" The men probably argue that a sprinkler wastes water. But, deep down, the real reason is that it gives the men an excuse to get out of their messy house full of hungry, screaming kids at 5:00 p.m.

One afternoon, I was watering my front lawn by hand when I noticed that *every other* neighbor was doing the same thing. Suddenly, one of the neighbors ran inside and came back out with a six-pack of beer to share with the other men. So now all of us men are standing in front of our houses, watering our lawns, drinking beer, and making small talk.

After a while, our wives start coming out to investigate what's taking us so long. When they see us drinking beer, they go inside and come back out with a bottle of wine. After some more time, the children start coming out of the houses to see what's going on and beg for food. So I order some pizza and invite the neighbors and their children into our backyard to eat. The neighbors and their children keep hanging out in our backyard and living room after dinner.

What happened here? We did our own creative version of *coffee, dinner, gospel*—except that it was *beer, pizza, gospel*. We were able to move from front yard conversations to backyard conversations—from public-space conversations to private-space conversations.

We need to look for our own creative ways to do hospitality. For many of us, the traditional forms of hospitality are impossible. Maybe we're still living at home with our parents. Or maybe we're living in the back of a car. Who knows? But that's where we can find work-arounds. We can order coffee for them and then pay for it—our treat! Or we can turn up at someone's place with a pizza. Or we can bake a cake and share it. In all of these examples, we still end up creating a space where we eat and drink together. And, ultimately, sharing food allows us to connect, relate, and talk.

Hospitality is costly. It costs time, effort, and money. It's a form of generosity. But hospitality gives us *social capital*. It allows us to earn our friends' trust so we can talk about things that matter. And if we've been generous to them, then they will most likely reciprocate by listening to our views, even if they don't agree with what we're saying. Hospitality also makes the host *vulnerable*—we're opening up our private homes to our guests. But in doing so, hospitality invites the guests to be vulnerable in return. This is a safe space where they can talk about private matters that are weighing on their hearts.[18]

Evangelism in the Workplace

The workplace has changed. These days, people try to get to work as early as possible to beat traffic. They skip coffee breaks. They eat lunch at their desk. They rush out at the end of the day to beat rush hour traffic and then pick up their children. How does *coffee, dinner, gospel* work in this environment?

Try this. Around 10:00 a.m., offer to do a coffee run—your treat. (Remember, hospitality is costly!) As you hand your coworkers their coffee, they will have to talk to you. This is where you make small talk. Then offer to do a lunch run—again, your treat! Now as you hand your coworkers their lunch, they're going to have to talk to you again—this time for a bit longer. This is where you can ask them how they're doing.

Hospitality takes creativity and sacrifice, but the conversation opportunities it creates are worth the effort.

It Really Works

In my ministry with City Bible Forum, I often get asked to give evangelistic talks in a variety of settings. A few years ago, City Bible Forum invited me to give a series of talks at lunchtime in a city pub. The organizers had gone to a lot of effort to promote the event. They told the Christian workers to invite their work friends to come along and hear my talks. It should've been an easy invitation. The venue was great. The talk titles were catchy. But the numbers were disappointing. You could have swung an elephant in that pub and not hit anyone.

So the organizers decided to add the secret sauce of evangelism. They asked the Christian attendees to do *coffee, dinner, gospel* with their non-Christian work friends and then invite them to the next City Bible Forum event.

It worked. Two years later, City Bible Forum invited me to give a breakfast talk at a café in that same city. This time, the venue was packed. It was standing room only. I had to stand on a bar stool to be seen and heard. And easily one-third of the crowd were non-Christians, happy to come to breakfast and hear a Christian speaker talk about Jesus.

I asked the organizers what they thought the difference was between this event and the previous one two years earlier. They replied, *"Coffee, dinner, gospel."*

Listen

The Golden Rule of Evangelism: Evangelize the Same Way You Want to Be Evangelized

I'm a classic example of a *loud* introvert. I do a lot of up front public speaking, and I'm great for funny stories at parties. But I need a lot of quiet time alone to recharge and recover from any face-to-face time with people.

A few years ago, I sat down for a two-to-three-hour flight on my way to give a talk to hundreds of people on how to tell their friends about Jesus. I needed some alone time on the plane to recharge for this event. But before I could put on my headphones (which is the international symbol for "please do not talk to me"), the man next to me asked whether I was traveling for business or pleasure.

"Business," I replied.

He probed, "Oh, what sort of business?"

"I'm in Christian ministry," I replied. "I'm going to give a talk about Jesus from the Bible." Then, to break the stunned silence that followed, I asked, "Do you have a faith?"

The man replied, "When I was a teenager in South Africa, I checked out Christianity. That's when I found out it was a front for hate crimes against gay people."

I anxiously started sorting through the countless responses that popped into my head. Which answer should I give? Where should I go from here?

This situation happens to me all the time. The issue is that talking about what you do for work is classic small-talk material. But when your answer is that you work full-time in Christian ministry, you drag the conversation from the *interests* and small-talk layer to the *worldviews* layer way before you and the person you are talking with are ready for it.

It's tempting to ask something like, "How blue has the sky been lately?" to bring the conversation back into the safe territory of small talk. But I've learned that asking a question like, "Do you have a faith?" is a good test to see whether they're comfortable with staying in the worldviews layer.

Then, no matter how they reply, I respond with, "Wow! Tell me more." I ask questions to invite them to keep sharing. And then I *listen*.

This technique reflects the Golden Rule of evangelism that Elmer John Thiessen explores in *The Scandal of Evangelism*: Evangelize the same way that you want to be evangelized.[19] Probably the most important way we can do this is by listening to the other person talk first.

Lessons in Listening

Two key experiences taught me the value of listening. The first one took place many years ago, when I was in college.

Some Jehovah's Witnesses knocked on my door, wanting to talk to me about God, Jesus, and salvation. I happily agreed, and we met for a total of six times over the course of six weeks.

The conversations were frustrating. Every time I said something, the woman replied with a pre-rehearsed monologue that lasted five to ten minutes. If I said something she didn't have a pre-rehearsed answer to, she'd look in the index of her red book, turn to the appropriate page, and read the prewritten response back to me.

It didn't feel like dialogue. This woman wasn't listening to anything I was saying. She was merely using my words to launch into what she wanted to say. As a result, I never felt *heard*, so I stopped listening.

That brings me to lesson number one on how *not* to evangelize: Unless our friends feel *heard*, they cannot listen to us, no matter how hard they try.

The second experience happened just last year. When I told my Uber driver that I work in Christian ministry, he immediately got angry with me. He was a Muslim who thought that Christianity was wrong. He launched into a monologue about why Christians are wrong in their beliefs. I never got a word in. (To top it off, I suspect he was responsible for my losing my five-star passenger rating.)

I was frustrated because the Uber driver was *wrong* about Christianity. He was misinformed. He was presenting horrible caricatures of what I believed. He had a distorted view of my faith and religion. But worst of all, he wasn't interested in listening to anything I might say in response—so I stopped listening to anything he was saying. I simply tuned out.

And that brings me to lesson number two on how *not* to evangelize: If we're not listening to our friends, then they won't be listening to us. They will tune us out.

If we want to tell our friends about Jesus, we must first learn the art of listening.

Practicing Active Listening

Many years ago, I faced a major life decision. I visited a lot of friends and asked for their advice. And they gave me their advice. They talked and talked. It took me a while to figure out why these visits were so frustrating. I asked for their advice, and they gave it to me. Isn't that what I wanted? It turns out that what I really wanted was to be *heard*. I wanted someone to talk to and someone to listen to me.

The key to having a good conversation is actually getting the other person to do most of the talking. A counselor friend of mine, James Veltmeyer, taught me that there are three forms of listening:

1. The first form is where you listen, but you're really just waiting for your own turn to say what you want to say. This isn't listening. It *looks* like you're listening, but you're not.
2. The second form is where you listen but you're working out how to argue against them, how to show

them why they're wrong, or what advice you're going
to give them. Once again, this isn't real listening.
3. The third form is real listening. Here you really are
   just letting them talk while you listen.

James told me his technique for practicing the third
type of listening—real listening—is simply to *not* talk.
If there's a long, uncomfortable pause in the conversation, take a sip from your drink. This is a nonverbal
signal to the other person that it's their turn to start
talking again.

I was on the receiving end of this technique when I
saw a professional counselor, and I can tell you this: it's
effective. My counselor spent more than 90 percent of each
session letting me talk. Occasionally, she chipped in with a
few of her insights. But for most of the time, she let me talk
freely. Whenever I stopped talking, she would take a drink,
and I would keep talking.

And that's what we're trying to do: invite our friends to
keep talking. But while they're talking, we need to remember to *listen*. When we're actively listening, we are trying
to do three things:

- *hear:* be able to demonstrate that we've *heard* what
  our friends are saying
- *understand:* be able to demonstrate that we've
  understood what our friends are saying by
  summarizing their words in our own words,
  showing that we've engaged in some sort of analysis
  of what they've been saying

- *feel:* be able to demonstrate that we empathize with our friends' emotions by describing what they are *feeling*

I like to joke with my male friends that it's everything we were taught in pre-marriage classes on how to manage conflict with our wives. For example, my wife says to me, "You're not doing the dishes enough." I can repeat her words to her: "From what I *hear* you saying, I'm not doing the dishes enough." Then I should summarize her words to demonstrate that I understand the bigger issue: "I *understand* I'm not doing my share of the house duties." Finally, I should empathize by speaking her emotions back to her: "Oh, that must make you *feel* disrespected. Have I heard you correctly?" A final step is to ask, "What can I do to restore *trust* in the relationship?"

If we put this "active listening" into practice in a real conversation, it might look like this. Imagine we've allowed our friends to talk at length about their views on same-sex marriage. When they're finished, we might find ourselves saying, "From what I *hear* you saying, you're very much for same-sex marriage. I *understand* how for you this is a matter of justice and equality. So you must *feel* angry when you hear that Christians might not share your point of view. It's going to take a lot before you *trust* Christians. Have I heard you correctly?"

When we actively listen in this way, our friends will feel heard. We will have connected with them emotionally. We know what viewpoint our friends are coming from, and we can talk to them accordingly. We have also earned enough capital to be able to speak. Our friend might ask us for our thoughts. Or we might politely ask, "Would you like me to respond?" And if our friend feels that they've been *heard*, *understood*, and *empathized* with, they will be open to hearing from us.[20]

Developing Realistic Expectations

I recently spent two weeks as a patient in the hospital. To pass the time, I watched several of Aaron Sorkin's movies—*A Few Good Men*, *Molly's Game*, and *The American President*. These movies don't have gunfights, car chases, or a big CGI (computer-generated imagery) fight scene at the end. But they do have dramatic tension that climaxes in a stirring speech from the lead actor.

The speech is the pinnacle of the movie. The speech knocks away all opposition. It is the "drop the mic" moment. But the speech is just as *unbelievable* as any Hollywood gunfight, car chase, or superhero CGI fight. In real life, it just doesn't happen that way.

When it comes to talking to our friends about Jesus, we often picture ourselves delivering a heroic and stirring speech to which they will respond by following Jesus. Or we picture ourselves answering every one of their questions with a silver bullet answer that removes all doubt. Or we catch them with a "gotcha!" sound bite that makes them realize how wrong they've been.

But I've found that conversations rarely happen that way. Usually I get to do a lot less talking and a lot more listening. And sometimes what I say matters a lot less than how I act. It all depends on the type of situation I'm in.

There are basically three situations where we tell people about Jesus, and each situation offers unique circumstances and opportunities to share.[21] Giving a public talk is not the same as talking to a stranger on a plane, and talking to a stranger on a plane is not the same as talking to your roommate about Jesus. Figuring out where we are on this spectrum helps us develop realistic expectations for our conversations.

PUBLIC TALK	STRANGER ON A PLANE	FRIENDS AND FAMILY
90–100% talking	50% talking	0–10% talking
0–10% listening	50% listening	90–100% listening
0–10% personal life	20–30% personal life	90–100% personal life
logical, linear, orderly	back-and-forth	organic, unstructured
one-off monologue	one-off conversation	multiple conversations

Situation #1: Public Talks

The first situation is where I'm invited to give a *public talk*—usually to an audience made up of both believers and nonbelievers. In my work with City Bible Forum in Australia, I often give talks in cafés, pubs, and conference rooms. My audience ranges from lawyers, traders, and accountants to high school students.

In this situation, I deliver a twenty-minute monologue and then answer questions. I do 90 to 100 percent of the talking. The audience knows very little about my personal life, apart from what I tell them. I am in control of the direction of the conversation. As a result, the talk is a logical progression of ideas in an ordered and coherent argument.

And because my talks are advertised as "Christian" talks, it gives me permission to talk about Jesus.

Situation #2: Encounters with Strangers

In the second situation, I find myself *talking to a stranger* —someone I will never meet again. These conversations typically take place on some sort of transportation—a car, bus, or plane.

In these situations, the stranger and I share the talking fifty-fifty. We go back and forth. The person knows very little about my personal life, but they might have some clues as to who I am based on what they've witnessed and how I've behaved. I have some control of the direction of the conversation, but so does the other person. As a result, we might talk about a variety of topics.

Situation #3: Interactions with Friends and Family

In the third situation, I am trying to talk to close *friends and family*, whom I will be with for the rest of my life. For me, this group includes the non-Christian doctors and nurses I work with, as well as close family members who are nonbelievers.

In this third situation, things are not straightforward. On the one hand, we have multiple opportunities to have conversations. On the other hand, if the conversation becomes unpleasant, things will be awkward between us whenever we see each other. Another difficulty is that if we've already had a few conversations about topics beyond small talk and found that we disagree, it's highly unlikely they will change their mind the next time the topic comes up.

The nature of the conversation we will have with family and friends will be very organic. There is no logical presentation of ideas. Instead, the conversation goes in all sorts of directions. Furthermore, we may find that the other person does 90 to 100 percent of the talking. Also, they know almost everything about our personal life.

The Unspoken Message

Recognizing where you and the nonbeliever you're speaking with are on the spectrum is important for more than just developing realistic expectations. According to the ancient Greeks, what you say is only the first of three components to the message you're delivering:

- *logos:* what I say
- *pathos:* the way I make you feel
- *ethos:* how I live

The makeup of my message differs, depending on which of the above three situations I'm in. When I give a public talk, there will be a lot of *logos* and *pathos* but little *ethos*. But when it comes to talking to close friends and family, *ethos* becomes a huge component. First Peter 3:1–2 captures this concept when it says that nonbelieving husbands can be "won over without words by the behavior of their wives, when they see the purity and reverence of [their] lives." In other words, when it comes to close, personal relationships, our *ethos* (how we live) may be much more persuasive than our *logos* (what we say).

The *ethos* plays a disproportionately large part in personal evangelism. What we say is important. But the more closely someone knows us, the more they will be persuaded by our way of life rather than merely by what we say.

The Gift of Reciprocation

When I invited the passenger next to me on the plane—the one who associated Christianity with hate crimes against gay people—to tell me more, he took me up on the offer.

For the duration of the flight, he talked and talked. Every time there was an uncomfortable pause, I sipped my drink and motioned for him to keep talking. As he talked, I practiced active listening.

After ninety minutes, he finally stopped talking. I seized the opportunity to show him I'd been listening: "From what I hear you saying, you have three objections against Christianity: (1) it's homophobic; (2) it's unscientific; and (3) all religions are the same anyway. Have I heard you correctly?"

I had, and when I asked if he would like me to respond, he said yes.

Social interactions tend to be governed by unspoken rules of reciprocation. If I ask you what you did on the weekend, you return the favor and ask me what I did on the weekend. If I let you talk for one minute, you let me talk for one minute. If I let you talk for ten minutes, you let me talk for ten minutes.

The man on the plane followed these unspoken reciprocation rules. Because I had let him talk for ninety minutes without interrupting him, he let me talk for the next sixty minutes without interruptions. Afterward, he thanked me for a great conversation. "You made that plane ride go so quickly!" he exclaimed.

I replied, "Thank you!" but inside I was cheekily grinning, "Not for me it didn't." I was exhausted from having done so much talking—but I got that chance only because I had done so much listening first.

Tell a Better Story[22]

Make Them Wish That Christianity Is True

Ethan was born, bred, and raised in Wisconsin in the US of A. He fit all the stereotypes—raised on a farm, cheering for the Green Bay Packers, driving a pickup, born into a Christian family, attending the church on Main Street, and helping lead youth group on Friday nights.

Ethan was keen to break out of the mold and explore the world. He wanted to expand his horizons, travel, and learn about other cultures. He got his opportunity in his second year of college when his application to transfer to a university in Sydney, Australia, was accepted.

After months of paperwork and errands, Ethan stepped off the plane and walked out of Sydney Airport. He couldn't wait to check out the beaches and learn to surf. Maybe he would sign up for the university rugby team. He wanted to buy a car and learn how to drive on the other side of the road. By the end of this college year, he wanted to be able to say he was an "Aussie."

But when Ethan walked onto the university campus, he got his first shock. There were Asian students *everywhere*. What was going on? Ethan hadn't realized that Australia is geographically located in Asia and has had a huge influx of Asian immigrants.

Ethan got his second shock when he walked into the lecture hall for his first meeting with a Christian group on campus. Ethan felt like he was the only Anglo there. The majority of the students in the group were Asian, but there were also Africans and South Americans. The Anglos were definitely in the minority.

What was going on?

Two Different Stories

Christianity is exploding right now. Thousands upon thousands of people are converting to Christianity in major world areas—Asia, Africa, South America, and the Middle East. But you wouldn't know this if you only live in a Western country—particularly the United States, United Kingdom, Canada, or Australia. In these countries, Christianity seems to be rapidly in decline.

What is going on? Why does the good news of Jesus have so much more cultural traction among Asians than among Anglos? Here is one possible factor: Asians and Anglos have been telling a different story of Jesus.[23]

The Asian Conversion Story

Sophia is an Asian American. She was born in Taiwan and came to the United States with her parents when she was a senior in high school. Her parents found a thriving Asian American Christian community in Houston—and soon the whole family believed in Jesus. Sophia is so glad she and her parents found Jesus.

Up until then, Sophia and her Asian parents lived in fear of evil spirits. Their life was a prison of superstitious rituals—which affected everything from choosing a house based on the number in the address and how to orient their furniture to what foods to eat and even how to address their parents. They were literally afraid of the dark. They were also trapped in the endless cycle of the need to impress relatives and friends. The endless drive for status, honor, and success. The endless need for fortune, wealth, and expensive cars. The endless expectation to study to become a doctor or lawyer—anything else would bring shame and dishonor.

But Jesus has set them free from all of that. They are now free from the fear of evil spirits. They are liberated from the bondage of superstitious rituals. They are set free from the endless need to impress. Sophia is now free to pursue a career that makes her happy. Jesus is perfect, so she doesn't need to pretend to be perfect. Jesus has washed away her shame. She has all the status, security, and honor she needs in Jesus.

Sophia feels sorry for her Asian friends who still haven't found Jesus. They are so enslaved and miserable. She wishes they could find Jesus and be as free as she is now. Sophia is so glad her parents found Jesus!

The Western Deconversion Story

Amy is an Anglo-American. She was born in Michigan. Her great-grandparents came to the United States from Sweden and were founding members of the local Protestant church. Amy's parents were once churchgoing,

Bible-believing Christians, but they stopped believing in Jesus many years ago. Amy is so glad her parents have stopped believing.

When they believed in Jesus, Amy and her parents lived in fear of breaking the Ten Commandments. Their life was a prison of religious rituals that affected everything—whether they could do laundry on Sunday, watch *The Simpsons*, date, or even wear leggings. They were trapped in an endless cycle of needing to impress their religious relatives and friends. Amy had to go to Sunday school and church on Sundays, youth group on Friday nights, and choir on Saturdays. She was forced to obey outdated views on sex, dating, and marriage. She was expected to go on mission trips to build orphanages on spring break. Anything else would bring shame and dishonor.

But Amy has been *set free* from all of this. Because she and her parents stopped believing in Jesus, they are now free from the fear of hell and punishment. They are liberated from the bondage of religious rituals. No more Sunday school, church, youth group, or choir. Amy can sleep in on Sundays. She doesn't need to obey authority figures, like her pastor. She is free to date whomever she wants and have sex whenever she wants. She can do whatever makes her happy.

Amy feels sorry for her old friends who are still trapped in church. They are so enslaved and miserable. She so wishes they could be as free as she is now. Amy is so glad she and her parents stopped believing in Jesus.

Can you see what's happened? Jesus is a different story

for Sophia than he is for Amy. For Sophia, who comes from a pre-Christian culture, Jesus offers freedom. But for Amy, who comes from a post-Christian culture, Jesus means the loss of freedom. This is one of the reasons we're seeing such an influx of converts to Christianity in Asia and a decline in Western countries.

The Western Story Line

Western culture is telling us a story that goes something like this: We once believed in God, fairies, and unicorns. But as we became more and more *enlightened*, we became rational and stopped believing in the supernatural. And so if we can leave behind our past superstitious beliefs and realize we're only physical atoms and molecules, then we can be free to be who we really are. The only thing holding us back are those who still haven't gotten with the program—that is, religious people who still believe in God, who continue to oppress us with their outdated beliefs, traditions, and morals. But if we can courageously be true to ourselves, we will discover the authentic selves within, and we can discover and pursue our full potential. chase our dreams, and refuse to let anyone else tell us who to be. More than this, this is the arc of history—i.e., humankind will become more and more free to pursue happiness on their own terms. And so we can either join the *progressives* along this story line or be left behind on the "wrong side of history."[24]

There are many positives in this story line. Many of us are who we are because of this story line. We didn't have to follow in our parents' footsteps and do the same job they did; instead, we could choose to do what we loved. We didn't have to stay in the town of our birth; instead, we were free to move to another town for study or work. We didn't have to marry someone from our own tribe or race; instead, we could choose our own romantic partners.

But this story line is also an over-the-top Western narrative of rugged individualism, egalitarianism, and privilege. It's an example of Western cultural superiority and triumphalism. And it only works if we stay in our tiny Western bubble. Right now, secularism is actually *declining* all over the world—and Christianity is the fastest-growing religion. Millions and millions of people, especially in the *majority* world—Africa, Asia, and Latin America—are choosing to love, worship, and follow Jesus. So what are they seeing in Jesus that we in the West are missing? Perhaps it's time we rediscovered the Jesus of the Bible.

Let's forget about the Jesus we think we know or grew up with. Let's go to the Bible and discover the Jesus the rest of the world is coming to know. And if we have any problems with the Bible, maybe they are our *Western* cultural objections, which the rest of the world just doesn't have. If we think Christianity is a tool of oppression, that is also probably only our Western presuppositions, because the rest of the world is discovering a freedom that comes from knowing the Jesus of the Bible.

God's Better Story For Us

When we were in the period of Christendom, the story of guilt and forgiveness connected with Martin Luther in the 1500s and our grandparents in the 1900s. During this period of Christendom, it was a *better story* of freedom. But to people in the *post-Christian* West, this same story sounds like one of power, oppression, and enslavement. It's the same story, but our post-Christian friends don't hear it the same way our Christendom ancestors did.

Fortunately, in the Bible, God gives a huge variety of stories, images, emotions, and metaphors designed to reach each and every person exactly where they are and connect with them emotionally, culturally, and existentially. No matter who your friends are and what they've been through, the Bible has a story about Jesus that will speak to them.

- If your friends are burdened by guilt and need forgiveness, tell them the story of Jesus and the tax collector who is justified by God (Luke 18:14).
- If your friends are burdened by shame and need restoration, tell them the story of Jesus cleansing and restoring a bleeding woman (Luke 8:48).
- If your friends feel impure and need to be clean, tell them that Jesus will cleanse them and wash away their sins (Hebrews 9:14).
- If your friends are enslaved by the worship of idols, tell them the story of Jesus inviting himself into Zacchaeus's home and setting him free from the power his wealth had over him (Luke 19:10).

- If your friends feel far from God, tell them how God the Father welcomes us as his children into his home (Luke 15:21–24).
- If your friends are wandering and lost, tell them how Jesus is the shepherd who will seek, find, and save them (Luke 15:1–7).
- If your friends are disconnected from God, tell them how Jesus is the vine, and we are his branches—we dwell in him, and he dwells in us (John 15).
- If your friends are restless and exhausted, tell them how Jesus will give them rest (Matthew 11:28).
- If your friends live in fear of evil spirits, tell them the story of Jesus driving out demons, who tremble and flee from him (Luke 4:31–36).
- If your friends are empty, outcast, broken, and unfulfilled, tell them about how Jesus offers the shamed, outcast, broken Samaritan woman living water that will overflow into eternal life—a full, filled, and fulfilled life (John 4).
- If your friends are afraid of death and the afterlife, tell them about Jesus raising Lazarus from the dead (John 11).
- If your friends feel they have let God down too many times, tell them how Jesus restores Peter, who disowned him three times (John 21).
- If your friends are burdened by the need to be perfect, tell them about the Pharisee who when he recognizes his need to humble himself before God, will be exalted by God (Luke 18:14).
- If your friends' lives are fractured, dysfunctional, and broken, tell them how Jesus grants peace to a troubled,

sinful woman who washes his feet with her tears, hair, and perfume (Luke 7:48–50).

- If your friends don't have any purpose or direction, tell them they can follow Jesus and be part of his mission (Luke 9:23).
- If your friends' lives are empty and self-absorbed, tell them they can die to their ambitions and live for the one who dies for us (Luke 9:23–26).
- If your friends are feeling undervalued and disrespected, tell them how Jesus welcomes and blesses children who had been rebuked for trying to see him (Mark 10:13–16).

No matter where your friends are—culturally, emotionally, and existentially—the Bible has a story about Jesus that will connect with them.

Ditch the Christian Jargon

Missionaries working in other cultures and languages have this classic principle: "What you say is not what they hear"—that is, what we say has one meaning to us, but in a different culture it can have a different meaning. There are countless examples of how certain words and symbols have acquired new meanings in the last few decades—words like *awful*, *gay*, and *thong*. We can insist on faithfully using these words and symbols and risk being misunderstood, or we can use new and different words to communicate the same intended meaning. For example, we can say "inspirational" instead of "awful," "happy" instead of "gay," and "flip-flops" instead of "thongs."

A few years ago, I went to an evangelistic outreach dinner. A Christian woman got up and shared her conversion story, which basically went like this: "I used to do my own thing. I was a rebel against God. But now I submit to Jesus, who is my king."

She used all the words and symbols we've been coached to use when we explain the gospel. Phrases and words like *do my own thing*, *rebel*, *submit*, and *king* used to mean one thing in Christendom. But in a post-Christian culture, they have a different meaning. Our culture praises *doing my own thing* and *rebelling* as good, brave, and noble things to do! And we associate words like *submit* and *king* with oppression. So when we use these words to describe our Christian experience, we're portraying Christianity as an oppressive institution that will impose its artificial constructs on you and take away your freedom.

The issue is that, within Christendom, we developed a system of Christian jargon that was precise and efficient in explaining what we believe and do. But outside of Christendom, these words and phrases have completely different meanings.

Other fields have jargon too. Consider the field of medicine. Doctors have medical jargon that is very precise and efficient: *shock, chronic, acute, schizophrenic*. If I say any of these words to another doctor, they will know exactly what I mean. But if you're not a health care professional and I say these things to you—"the patient is in shock"; "the pain is chronic"; "it's an acute abdomen"; or "this is very schizophrenic"—you will hear the *wrong* meaning because in the everyday world these words have completely different meanings.

Good doctors learn how to communicate to you in your language rather than in their own medical, textbook jargon. We as Christians need to learn to do the same.

Some examples of Christian jargon words are *sin, rebel, born-again, submit, repent, salvation, redemption,* and *king.* To our Christian ears, these words are efficient and have a precise meaning. We often feel we need to use these exact words if we're going to do the gospel justice. But these words have a totally different meaning to our post-Christian friends.

We need to rethink the traditional words and symbols we've been using to tell our friends about Jesus and come up with new ones. It's time to become a blank slate and start all over again. Our post-Christian friends are misunderstanding what we're really trying to say—so we need to find a new way to communicate the Christian truths in which we believe.

A Jargon-Free Gospel Message

Here's one of my go-to explanations of the gospel for my non-Christian friends:

There's more to this life than what we can see and touch. We are more than just atoms and molecules. We are more than just another species of life on this planet. We are more than just a blip in the timeline of this universe. We are more than the sum of our parts. We are part of something bigger.

But what is this exactly? It's this: There's a God who loves us, made us, and saved us. And now we get to be part of his story. Every day is a day when I live for Jesus because he lives for me. Every day is a day when I can journey with Jesus and bring his love, mercy, and justice to this planet.

If this is true, then we are set free from our empty and self-absorbed lives. We are set free to admit that everything is not okay right now. The person you see on the outside is not the person on the inside. I'm not the person I pretend to be. But that's okay. Because Jesus is perfect, so I don't have to pretend to be perfect anymore. Jesus' Spirit lives in me right now, and he loves me just the way I am.

But Jesus loves me too much to leave me the way I am. Every day is a day when he makes me more and more into the person he wants me to be. Every day is a day when I can become my full potential—not through my plan for myself, but through God's plan for me. Every day is a day when I can be everything God has made me to be.

Explaining Jesus to a Post-Christian World

In the Bible, Jesus and his followers appropriated symbols and language from their audience's culture to explain the gospel to them. For instance, Jesus is the "Word" (*logos*) who has become flesh. Jesus is the "shepherd." Jesus is the "light" to a man born blind. Jesus offers "living water" to a woman looking for water.

We can follow Jesus and his followers' example when we talk about Jesus with our friends. Here are some of the ways I try to explain Jesus to my post-Christian friends.

- "There is a God who loves us and made us. But we haven't been worshiping and honoring him."
- "Jesus died for us and now lives for us. Now I live for him as he lives for me."
- "I no longer have to be self-absorbed and unfulfilled. I can now be part of God's bigger story for my life."
- "I'm loyal to Jesus, and I get to be part of Team Jesus."
- "I get to be part of Jesus' mission for this world. Every day is a day when I can bring his love, mercy, and justice to this world."
- "God loves me just the way I am. But he loves me too much to leave me the way I am. Every day is a day when I become more and more like Jesus."

When I listen to my friends and hear where they're coming from—culturally, emotionally, and existentially—I can appropriate their language and show them that Jesus is the one they're looking for. I'm using their heart language to show them that Jesus is God's *better story* for them. It's exactly what Jesus did for the woman at the well when he offered living water (John 4). It's what Jesus did when he offered light to the man born blind (John 9). It's what John did when he called Jesus the "Word" (*logos*) in John 1.

Shibboleths and Evangelism

Australian evangelist John Chapman has a story of when he preached a gospel message at a church. Afterward, someone complained to him, "You didn't mention *the blood*." I had a similar experience. After I preached a gospel message at a church, someone complained to me, "You didn't use the word *repent*." I was confused, because I had talked about doing a U-turn and returning to God. But to this person, unless I used the exact word *repent*, I hadn't properly explained the gospel.

These stories show that some Christians have *shibboleths*—key words that signal orthodoxy and loyalty—when they judge a gospel message. These Christians act like gatekeepers. Until they hear their shibboleths, they won't grant that you have preached the gospel.

I can think of a few things to say in reply. First, we can communicate ideas without using the exact same words. For example, Jesus was able to explain "sin" in many of his parables (e.g., the Wedding Banquet, the Rich Fool, the Rich Man and Lazarus) without using the word *sin*.

Second, we can't say everything in our early attempts at telling the gospel. Even Jesus has to leave a lot out. Whenever Jesus meets someone, he doesn't say everything.

This is why we don't evangelize by reciting the Apostles' Creed to our friend. Or by giving them a printed copy of our church's statement of faith.

In the end, our evangelistic efforts are aimed at

outsiders. We are giving them an entry point to the gospel. This is different from a statement of faith—essentially a long list of shibboleths!—which acts as an exhaustive set of necessary beliefs for *insiders*.

Third, the gospel is no less than our shibboleths—for example, the blood, sin, the cross, justification, hell, and so on—but it is also more than just our shibboleths. That's why God gave us sixty-six books of the Bible and not just a four-page evangelistic tract. This means we can choose from a large variety of starting points to introduce our friend to the gospel.

Evangelism on the Road

When I meet people out in the world, I look for opportunities to find what story of Jesus they need to hear. For instance, one time after I told my Uber driver I work full-time in Christian ministry, it resulted in a conversation that was more fruitful than usual. After I asked my driver if she had faith, she explained that she was raised Catholic but doesn't believe anymore. She defined herself as "spiritual." I asked her to tell me more—and she did. "I believe it's about making a difference," she said. "I like to look for beauty everywhere. I especially find beauty in sunsets at the beach." I kept asking questions, and she reciprocated.

Eventually the conversation shifted to our home life,

and I told her I brew beer as a hobby. "Can you do that as a minister?" she asked.

This provided me the perfect opening to tell her the story of Jesus turning water into wine (John 2). I explained that this story shows what life with Jesus will be like both now and in the life to come: It will be a full and fulfilled life. Then, to show her I had been listening when she talked, I said, "You told me earlier that you enjoy beauty. Where do you think beauty comes from? It comes from God. He deliberately made this world beautiful so we can enjoy it."

Eventually the driver started asking me questions about things she really wanted to know the answer to—in this case, the meaning of the word *grace*. This is how it usually goes.

Another time, I was chatting with the passenger next to me on the plane. When I asked her if she has faith, she explained that she used to, but now she just goes to church once or twice a year to make her parents happy. She told me that church feels dry, dead, and boring. She particularly took issue with the crucifix at her parents' church. The image of Jesus dying on the cross made her feel like she was at a funeral.

I told her that not all churches are that way. At my church, the cross is empty. Jesus is alive. We're running a celebration. Church is actually all about worshiping and celebrating Jesus, who is alive and whose Spirit is living inside us right now.

"Did you know that when Jesus was alive on earth, people complained that he was doing too much celebrating?"

I asked. "They called him a glutton and a drunkard. People once asked Jesus why he wasn't fasting and praying and being mournful. Do you know what he said? He said, 'The bridegroom is here.' He's alive and with us. Now is the time to be celebrating not mourning, to be singing, dancing, eating, and drinking."

This led to her asking what I think happens to us after we die.

Both of these conversations began with me listening and asking questions to give the other person permission to talk. But they ended with them asking me questions about my faith and giving me permission to talk. They were *inviting* me to tell them the gospel message.

Manger, Cross, King

Sharing the gospel message with our friends can feel overwhelming. What if we leave out something important? It's helpful to have a simple outline to follow. Tim Keller encourages Christians to adopt a gospel outline similar to the one I present here. The bullet points are *manger* (incarnation), *cross* (atonement), *king* (restoration).[25] As we follow this outline, we put it in words that our friends would use and understand.

1. *Manger:* We can begin by saying something about how God sent us his Son Jesus. He was a first-century Jewish man who walked around Galilee speaking Aramaic. Jesus was one of us—a human.

79

2. *Cross:* Next we can say something about how Jesus died for us in our place. If we believe this, then God will wash away our guilt and shame.

3. *King:* Finally, we can talk about how each person can choose to be loyal to Jesus and become part of his team to spread his love, mercy, and justice. One day, Jesus will come again and set up his kingdom here on earth. On that day we get to be with Jesus forever.

I use this outline to answer the question that the person asks me. For example, to the Uber driver's question, "What is grace?" I answered:

Christians believe that God sent us his Son Jesus to be one of us. Jesus died on a cross to save us. But he rose from the dead, and he's going to come again to fix everything up. So *grace* is how everything we have is a gift from God—because he is generous; not because we have earned it. This frees us from having to pretend we're perfect. This frees us from being proud. This frees us to be generous to others. We live life knowing we are always loved by God, no matter what. That's grace.

When the passenger next to me on the plane asked, "What happens to us after we die?" I said:

Christians believe that God sent us his Son Jesus to be one of us. Jesus dies on a cross to save us. But he rose from the dead, and that means if we trust in Jesus, we will also live with him after we die. And one day Jesus is going to come again and set up his kingdom here on this earth. We get to be part of that kingdom. So, yes, I do believe we don't stay dead. There is life after death.

The interesting thing is that because I'm using my gospel outline *to answer their question*, suddenly the story of Jesus is more believable to them. Crazy stuff like Jesus being the Son of God, Jesus rising from the dead, and us rising from the dead doesn't sound weird when it's my answer to their question.

Telling Your Story as a Story

A powerful way of telling the gospel is to tell your friend the difference that Jesus has made in your life. This can flow quite naturally in a conversation, especially if you have asked them about their faith. Your friend may quite naturally reciprocate and ask how you became a Christian. Or you can simply offer, "Would you like to know how I became a Christian?"

This is our opportunity to give them what is known in Christian jargon as our "testimony"—our story of either how we became a Christian or what God has been doing in our lives up until now. A story requires two elements: (1) events that have happened to us and (2) a storytelling grid by which the events are arranged.

Typically, our Christian testimonies have too much of

one element and not enough of the other. They tell you the events, but without a grid, so it becomes a rambling, incoherent sequence. Or they tell you a grid, but with no events, so it becomes an abstract, formulaic presentation. I used to teach at a Bible college where the students often had to share their testimonies at a church event. I used to joke that the testimonies sounded so similar that students could swap testimonies with each other and no one would notice. I was hearing a grid, but without events that marked the testimony as that person's particular testimony. They often sounded like, "I grew up in a Christian family—not that this makes me a Christian, but it helps—but at the age of sixteen, I had to make a decision for myself."

So how can we tell our story as a story? By using a storytelling grid to arrange the events in our lives.

Typically a story has these parts:

Part 1: Introduction
- The main *character*—a hero—is introduced.

The Mission
- A *mission* is defined.
- So that a *goal* can be achieved

Part 2: The Body
- The hero begins the *quest* to achieve the mission.
- But there are *obstacles* too big to overcome.

Bridge
- The hero has an "aha moment" when they *redefine* the goal
- and *recommit* to the mission, ready to launch into the climax . . .

Part 3: The Climax

- The hero *achieves* the mission.

Denouement

- We glimpse the hero in their new *normal* life.

We can see how this storytelling grid works in sports movies. In the *introduction*, we meet the heroes—usually a lovable team of misfits who are hopeless at football. We learn a bit about their characters. Soon the *mission* is defined. They have to win the state tournament. The goal is to save the orphanage. During the *body*, they hire an old, washed-up, alcoholic, has-been coach. This coach gets them closer and closer to the state tournament final. But just before the final game, their star quarterback breaks a leg, and the coach starts drinking again, and now it's going to be impossible to win the final. In the *bridge*, someone gives them a stirring speech, and they have an "aha moment." The goal isn't just to save the orphanage; this is also a chance for personal redemption. They recommit to the mission by training extra hard—with an accompanying training montage. In the final, in the *climax*, they achieve the mission by winning the game—in overtime, of course, by one point. They saved the orphanage. But they also proved to themselves that they are winners. In the *denouement*, we find out where the players and coach are now—Steve became a lawyer, Shawn became a professor, and Sheldon is a United States senator.

We also see this storytelling grid in the Gospels. In the *introduction*, we meet Jesus. His *mission* is defined when he is baptized by John the Baptist—it's to be the "lamb"—i.e., to die sacrificially on a cross. His goal is to take away the sins of the world. During the *body*, Jesus progressively achieves his mission by preaching, teaching, healing, and finally entering Jerusalem. But in Gethsemane, the burden seems too much for Jesus. In the *bridge*, Jesus prays and has an "aha moment." The goal is to do God's will. Jesus recommits to the mission. In the *climax*, Jesus dies on the cross. In the *denouement*, we have Jesus' postresurrection appearances to his disciples.

If we are to tell our story as story, we can apply this same storytelling grid. I've simplified it into this template:

I am _____

[**Introduction:** describe yourself]

My mission in life was _____

[**Mission:** state your mission]

Because I wanted to achieve _____

[**Goal:** what goal were you trying to achieve?]

So I _____

[**Body:** describe how you tried to achieve this mission]

But _____

[**Obstacle:** explain the problem of trying to fulfill this mission without God]

But Jesus _____

[**Bridge:** this is your "aha moment" of the gospel.

Explain how Jesus is your goal. Explain how Jesus achieves your mission for you.]

That's when I decided _____
[**Climax:** explain how you decided to follow Jesus]

So now I _____
[**Denouement:** explain what living with Jesus looks like in your life now]

After you've filled out this template, try to insert *examples* or *events* to flesh out each part.

Using this grid, my testimony could sound like this:

I am a firstborn Asian son who is a high achiever. My mission in life was to study hard and become a doctor. If I could become a doctor, it would give me status, self-worth, and security. For example, in elementary school, I always asked my teacher for more work—yes, I was *that* annoying kid in your class.

So I tried to achieve my mission by getting good grades. For example, in high school, while my friends were partying, I was busy studying. But the problem with being a high achiever is that it makes you proud and insecure at the same time. You need more and more achievements to be somebody in your own eyes. For example, once I was a doctor, it wasn't enough for my self-worth. I also had to become a surgeon to be somebody in the medical community and in my own eyes.

But Jesus came to give me all the status, self-worth, and security I needed. I had grown up in a Christian family and had known Jesus all my life. But I don't think I fully understood this until someone helped me read the Bible and showed me the bit where Jesus is perfect so I don't have to be perfect. God loves me just the way I am because of what Jesus has done. I didn't need to be a doctor with qualifications to earn God's love.

That's when I decided I didn't need to chase achievements to be secure. I didn't have to be proud of what I had done and yet insecure that I hadn't done enough. Instead, if I had Jesus, I could be humble and secure. Humble because it's Jesus who is perfect, not me. Secure, because my status was found in Jesus, not me.

So now I no longer chase achievements to be somebody. For example, a few years ago, I had to decide if I wanted to remain in full-time medicine. In the past, I needed to be a doctor to feel important—people at parties want to talk to you and bank managers want to lend you money! But I was able to leave full-time medicine because it no longer mattered what others thought of me. I was important in God's eyes. Jesus is perfect so I don't have to be perfect to be somebody in God's eyes.

Can you see how I can use this testimony instead of my previous standard "I grew up in a Christian family" testimony?

What about you? How could you give your testimony? The key moment is being able to answer the questions "Who am I?" "What is my mission?" and "What is my ultimate goal?" Once you work this out for yourself, the rest of the testimony should flow. But at the same time, these are the hardest questions to answer. When I asked my seminary students to do this exercise, they often sat staring at a blank page for an hour, repeatedly asking themselves, *Who am I?* What about you? Can you work this out for yourself?

But What If I Grew Up in a Christian Family?

People often ask me, "Were your parents Christian?" When I answer yes, they immediately stop listening. They are thinking, *Oh, that's why you're a Christian. You grew up in a Christian family*, and it invalidates whatever I'm about to say next.

So I like to reply that, yes, I did grow up in a Christian family, *but that makes it harder to be a Christian.* Because nobody wants to inherit their identity from their parents. Teens go out of their way to be the exact opposite of what their parents want. In the same way, when I grew up in a Christian family, there was no way I wanted to be a Christian because that's what mommy and daddy told me to be. I needed to believe the claims of Jesus and the Bible on their own merits, and not because of what my parents told me.

Discovering the Better Story of Jesus

Ethan couldn't believe how quickly his year of college in Australia went by. But he also couldn't believe how much the Christian group on campus had grown in the last year. Quite a few nonbelievers were checking out the group, staying, and becoming Christians. And this was true for both the Anglos and the Asians.

Ethan's experience is typical of many Christian groups on campuses right now. They are seeing many university students becoming Christians—both the Anglos and the Asians. But how is this possible? The media tells us that Christianity is in decline in the West. We hear stories of Christians deconverting from their faith, but never the other way around. So what is going on?

It all comes down to the story they are being told. Typically, Western university students think they've been told the better story already. They've been told they are unique, special, and precious. They've been taught to ignore what others tell them to be and instead chase their dreams. They're encouraged to be whoever they want to be, to be true to themselves, to do whatever makes them happy.

It's a great story. But it always falls apart. It's impossible to do what makes you happy all the time. They become tired of just existing, living from day to day. They need to live for something. They're hungry for purpose!

In Christ, they discover belonging. They find a tribe. And they find a *better story* than the one they have. They finally discover *why* they are here. They find a God who made them, loves them, and saves them. And they find a bigger story to live for than just for themselves. They are no longer alone in this universe. They have a reason to be here.

As someone who is Chinese, I often like to make a self-deprecating joke about Chinese tourists in Europe. Chinese tourists tend to stay on their tourist buses with other Chinese tourists, only speaking Chinese to each other and only venturing out of the bus to eat at Chinese restaurants—which they then complain about because the food isn't as good as the food back home. But someone pointed out that British tourists do the same thing, and so do American tourists.

As long as tourists stay in their bubbles, they will never see their own cultural presuppositions and biases. And they will never truly experience the host country's culture, language, peoples, and food.

Many in the West stay in their bubbles—with their preconceptions about Jesus, the Bible, and Christianity. But we can point this out to them and invite them to step out of their bubbles and experience the Jesus of the Bible on his own terms. And maybe they can see what the rest of the world has been seeing in Jesus—someone with a better story than the one they have right now.

Tell Them Stories about Jesus

Scratch Their Itching Ears with Jesus

Kevin's neighbor Irfan is the perfect neighbor. Irfan checks Kevin's mailbox when Kevin and his family are away on vacation. Irfan takes Kevin's trash bin off the street once it's been emptied by the garbage truck. Irfan gives Kevin oranges from his own tree. Irfan is the perfect neighbor.

Irfan is also Muslim. For a long time, Kevin has been trying to work out how to tell Irfan about Jesus. Kevin has done all the things I've recommended so far. He's introduced his Christian friends to Irfan. Kevin has gone to the mosque with Irfan. Kevin has had Irfan and his family to his house for dinner. Kevin has asked Irfan about his Muslim faith and tried to listen and to understand what Irfan is saying. Kevin has gone to Irfan's kids' fundraisers, concerts, and sports games.

But conversation still seems limited to the weather, sports, and television. Kevin feels trapped in the dreaded friend zone.

The Friend Zone

The friend zone is a common trope in movies and books. You have John, who is madly in love with Jane. But the feeling isn't mutual. Jane still views John as just a friend. This puts John in a tricky position. If he *overplays* his romantic intentions, he will drive her away. But if he *underplays* his romantic intentions, he will miss out on the opportunity to date her.

This is similar to the dilemma many of us face as Christians. How can we talk to our friends about Jesus? Right now, we're in a similar friend zone. We want them to be more than just our friends. We want them to also have the opportunity to know, love, and worship Jesus. But if we overplay this, we risk driving them away. They might never want to have another awkward conversation with us. But if we underplay this, our friends will never have the chance to hear about Jesus.

The Dilemma

This is the dilemma between *overfunctioning* and *underfunctioning*. These terms are common in family systems theory, which teaches that we and our relationships exist somewhere along a spectrum between over- and underfunctioning. We are looking for that Goldilocks sweet spot right in the middle. If we find this spot, we will have found our peace. But if we're nudged out of our sweet spot, we will be stressed.

For example, as a parent, if I neglect my children by being constantly absent in their lives, then I am underfunctioning. But if I do my children's science projects for them, then I am overfunctioning. Somehow, as a parent, I have to find the sweet spot right in the middle.

It's the same with telling our friends about Jesus. God has blessed us with great friends. We should enjoy our friends just for who they are—a good gift from a good God to enjoy—regardless of whether we get to tell them about Jesus. But at the same time, we should make the most of every opportunity God has given us to tell our friends about Jesus.

If I only see the friendship as a means to tell them about Jesus, then I'm overfunctioning. I'm trying to make something happen that might not be there. And I am using them as a means toward an end. Instead, I need to enjoy the friendship just for what it is—a gift from God.

On the other hand, if I don't try to tell them about Jesus, I'm underfunctioning. There will be times when I could have and should have tried to tell them about Jesus. These opportunities are given to me by God! I need to be a good steward of them.

So how can we get the balance right? Let me share some pointers that may help.

Ask a Nudge Question

It helps if we come out and ask a question that nudges the conversation into spiritual matters. Borrowing from chapter 3, here are some good questions to ask:

- Do you have a faith?
- What religion did your parents raise you with—and what was that like?

- What's the best thing about being an atheist (or Muslim, Buddhist, etc.)?[26]

If they're ready to talk, they will. Our job is to listen properly, hear, understand, and empathize with them. If we do this, they will return the favor and ask us about our faith.

Evangelize Like a Counselor

I find it interesting that when I was a seminary student in the twentieth century (yikes!), my evangelism professors were *preachers*. They taught us how to preach an evangelistic sermon in the style of Billy Graham. Thus the primary model of evangelism was a *sermon*, *talk*, or *monologue*.

But the more I think about it, I now think we should learn to evangelize like *counselors*. Counselors are skilled in asking the right questions. They steer their clients to talk out loud and discover the solutions for themselves. If we evangelize this way, our new model of evangelism will be a *conversation*.

Just Do It

Sooner or later, it's better if we just do it—just come out and tell them we're a Christian. But often we don't do this because, deep down, we're afraid of how they will react. We don't know if they'll be happy or sad, surprised or offended, calm or angry. It's something outside of our control. So what can we do?

Family systems theory is helpful here. The two key questions to ask ourselves in all relationships are these: (1) *What can I control?* (2) *What am I responsible for?* In other words, don't get anxious about what we're not responsible for. Don't stress about things we can't control. Instead, focus only on what we can control, and bear only the burden of what we're responsible for.[27]

For example, if I play the drums in an orchestra, I can control the drums. But I can't control the violins. I need to concentrate on playing the drums because that's what I am responsible for and what I can control. Similarly, if I play defense in football, I am responsible for guarding my opponent or zone. If an opponent I'm not guarding or in a zone I'm not defending gets the ball and scores, that's something out of my control. I should not hold myself responsible for that. As they say in American football, it wasn't my *assignment*.

In the same way, if we come out and tell our friend we're a Christian, their response is out of our control. It's something out of our area of responsibility. The way they react is *not our assignment*. If they are cool about it, then we rejoice. If they're angry about it or end the friendship, then we grieve. But we shouldn't feel guilty about their response.

So sooner or later, we should just do it—just come out and tell our friend that we're a Christian. In most cases, they will react better than we expected. By now we've built up enough trust and goodwill that they will accept our Christianity as part of who we are. And because most non-Christians don't know any Christians, it's good for them to realize they have a Christian friend inside their bubble of friends. And now that they know you're a Christian, they can come up to you and ask, "So what do Christians say about this?" It will open up *more* opportunities for conversations rather than less.

Tell Them a Story about Jesus from the Bible

Many years ago, I was on a bus in Tanzania. The man sitting next to me was a Muslim. He asked in broken English if I was a Christian. I said, "Yes." For the rest of that sixteen-hour bus trip, the man deliberately made my life miserable. He sat on my side of my seat, chain-smoked, and blew the smoke in my direction. To him, I had identified myself as his enemy and flown my fighting color; now he was doing the same.

Missionaries have since taught me that I shouldn't have immediately answered the man's question. Instead, I should have asked him, "What do you mean by *Christian*?" He might have said a Christian is an American who fights Muslims. I could have replied, "Oh, if that's what you mean by Christian, then that's not what I am. But I can tell you that I'm someone who belongs to Jesus."

Similarly, when we tell our friend that we're a "Christian," they often don't know what we mean by that.

If we tell our post-Christian friends *only* that we're a Christian, chances are they will not understand. Worse, they will associate us with whatever wrong ideas they have about Christianity. They may even see us as drawing an "us versus them" line in the sand. We can alleviate this confusion by asking a follow-up question like, "What do you think of when I say I'm a Christian?" or "What do you think I mean when I say I'm a Christian?"

A great way to show your friend what you mean when you say you're a Christian is to tell them a story about Jesus from the Bible. Most of our nonbelieving friends have no idea what's in the Bible. They may have some poor caricatures of what they think the Bible says, but they've never actually read or heard the Bible for themselves. But if we give them a chance to hear from the Bible, they will discover for themselves how fresh, disarming, and countercultural the Bible's message is. Moreover, telling them a story from the Bible allows them to *imagine* the Bible's worldview rather than merely giving them an *argument* to argue against.

Depending on the context, I may tell them the story of Jesus healing the paralyzed man lowered through the roof on a mat by his friends (Luke 5:17–26). Afterward, I may ask them, "Why would Jesus do that?" and see what my friend says. Or I may tell them the story of Jesus turning water into wine (John 2:1–12). I love this story because it's so disarming. *What on earth is Jesus doing, giving so much good wine to people who had already drunk enough?* So I ask my friend, "Why would Jesus do that?" I usually have a chance to explain: "Jesus partly did this to give us an image of what life is like with him in this life and in the life to come. So if you think that by following Jesus in this life you will miss out, you're wrong. It's actually the opposite. By *not* following Jesus in this life you will miss out." And then I see where the conversation goes from there.

Or sometimes I like to tell the story that Jesus tells about the Pharisee and the tax collector (Luke 18:9–14). Afterward, I explain that the Pharisee's prayer *today* would probably sound like this: "Dear God, I thank you that I'm better than most people. I drive a hybrid car and not a gas-guzzler. I give my money to charity. I don't cheat on my wife. I go to all of my children's plays, concerts, and awards nights. And I go to church twice on Sundays—both the traditional and contemporary services." Then I ask, "Why does he not get saved, according to Jesus?" I then have a chance to explain that, while we often think of sin as breaking laws, Jesus usually speaks of sin as being puffed up—being self-righteous or bragging. I can then explain that the tax collector got saved by humbling himself and trusting in God.

After telling them a story about Jesus, we can ask further questions and see where that takes us:[28]

- What did you like in that story?
- What questions do you have about that story?
- What does that story teach us about Jesus?
- What does that story teach us about people?
- If that story is true, what is God trying to teach you?

Become a Bible Page-Turner

We can also simply take our friends directly to the Bible to read stories about Jesus. Of course, the challenge here is not just that the Bible is foreign to our friends. The actual *form* of the Bible is scary to our friends—a big, thick, black, leather-bound book with thin pages and tiny writing. It's the stuff of horror movies. The *method* of reading the Bible is also very off-putting. Nobody wants to read out loud. It took me a long time to realize this.

In recent years, my colleagues at City Bible Forum have been using *The Word One to One* (www.theword121.com)— the gospel of John printed in a series of thin, faux-denim, contemporary-looking paperback booklets. Each booklet is only fifty pages, with large, friendly fonts. Each page has only three to five verses from the book of John, with some explanatory notes.

Our friend can read the whole of John's gospel by themselves. But it's unlikely that they're going to initiate this themselves. So we offer to come and "turn the pages" for them. Our friend reads the verses on the page for themselves. We read the explanatory comments. At the end of each page, we turn the page. It's brilliantly simple. The end result is that our friend reads the Bible for themselves; we answer whatever questions they have; and they get to take home a book of the Bible in an accessible format.

How to Invite Your Friend to Read the Bible

Richard Borgonon, who loves using *The Word One to One* with his friends, simply invites them to read the book of John: "The Bible has sold more copies than any other book in the history of printing. Haven't you always thought that one day you might try and read it? Don't you expect that it's probably got some good stuff in it for helping us how to live? Well, there is one book of the Bible—John—that is unique because it starts with a really helpful overview; in business it would be called an executive summary! This summary

---

is only eighteen sentences long, and I've got these great notes, which have gone global in no time at all, that will help you look at what it says. Can I buy you a coffee to look at this overview?"

After using *The Word One to One* to read John 1:1–18 with his friend, Richard then asks, "Did you enjoy that? Would you like to meet again to see what comes next?"

Taking the Leap

One night, Irfan and Kevin were kicking back on Kevin's patio and chilling over drinks and snacks. After talking about the weather, sports, and TV shows, Kevin decided to ask a nudge question: "My kids have been asked to write a school report on major world religions. One question they have to answer goes like this: *What would a Muslim find attractive about Christianity?* I'm not a Muslim, so I don't know how to answer that question. But you're a Muslim. What would you say?"

Irfan thought for a while. Finally he said, "I like how we all come from the same forefather, Abraham. We have a common ancestor. I think that's cool." Then Irfan paused and looked at Kevin, "What would *you* say?"

Kevin thought carefully. Then he took the leap. He explained that most other religions expect their followers to adopt the culture and language of the religion's founder, and that many expect followers to go somewhere sacred on a pilgrimage—but it's the opposite with Jesus. Jesus comes to us as a normal human being. We don't have to go to Jesus; he comes to us.

Then, recognizing that Irfan was listening and receptive, he explained more about Jesus and asked if he could read a story from the Bible with him. Irfan agreed, and together they began to read the gospel of John.

It was as simple as that.

Become Their Unofficial, De Facto Chaplain

You Are Their Connection with the Sacred

My friend Craig is a military chaplain. He spent a few years with his unit of soldiers when they were deployed in Afghanistan. There his unit experienced many of the tragedies of war. So he was often called on to conduct funerals, provide counseling, and comfort the soldiers.

The commanding officer of this unit was an atheist—a strict, outspoken nonbeliever. He had no time for religion or other such nonsense. One day, the commanding officer asked Craig to come into his office, close the door, and take a seat. The unit had gone through a few troubling weeks, and traumas and tragedies were still confronting them, leaving them raw and hurting. The commanding officer looked Craig in the eyes for a long time before finally saying, "I need you to pray for me." So Craig did.

My chaplain friends—military, hospital, or school—say this is very normal. They tell me our secular friends can be very firm in their nonbelief. But in a time of crisis, they will look to us to speak to them on behalf of God. They want us to make sense of what has just happened. They want us to connect them with something transcendent. They want us to give some meaning and coherency. Sometimes they even want us to perform a sacred ritual. Or sometimes it's something as seemingly small as a prayer.

How to Be a Chaplain

We can position ourselves into our non-Christian friends' lives as their unofficial, de facto chaplain.[29] Below are some characteristics of a chaplain you can adopt in your own life.

A Chaplain Is Wise

I recently hosted a barbecue for a bunch of friends. As we sat in my backyard enjoying the beef brisket and pulled pork, my guests admired my green, lush lawn. They began to ask for my advice on how to manage lawns. "What time of the year do you fertilize? How do you get rid of your weeds?" As I answered their questions, they were hanging on my every word.

My friend Marco had once been a professional landscaper. He also began to offer advice. He explained the different types of grass, what time of day was best for watering the lawn, and what height the lawn should be mowed at various times of the year. His knowledge and experience in lawn care were evident. Soon he had all of us, including me, hanging on his every word.

The conversation at this barbecue began in the layer of interests—*describing* my lawn. It soon moved to a different category, as we began *prescribing* what to do with the lawn.

But to say we were in the layer of values doesn't seem to be accurate. It was something slightly different. We were in a unique layer of conversation called *wisdom*.

In the Old Testament, we find wisdom in what is traditionally called the wisdom literature—Job, Psalms, Proverbs, Ecclesiastes, and Song of Songs. In the New Testament, we find similar teachings, such as Jesus' Sermon on the Mount, Paul's advice in the second half of his letters, and the book of James.

Knowing God's wisdom is more than knowing what's true or false, right or wrong; it's knowing what is most *apt* in a particular circumstance. For example, sometimes the wise thing to do is to answer a fool according to their folly (Proverbs 26:5), but at other times the wise thing to do is to *not* answer a fool (26:4). So which is it? Here the question is not so much what is true or right but what is wise.

So how can we know this wisdom? In one sense, wisdom is part of God's *general* truth—freely available both to Christians and non-Christians. This is because God has programmed his wisdom into his creation (Proverbs 8) so everyone can see it. As a result, those who observe God's wisdom in his creation will be able to live according to God's design and prosper.

But in a deeper sense, we can argue that the wisdom sections of the Bible only make sense if we've been saved by Jesus. This is because wisdom is part of God's *special* truth—for those already inside God's family. After all, the wisdom literature itself says that the "fear of the LORD is the beginning of wisdom" (Proverbs 9:10). To know Jesus is to know God's wisdom (1 Corinthians 1:24).

Christians should be known not just by our love (John 13:35) and ethics (1 Peter 4:4), but also by our *wisdom* (Colossians 4:5). Interestingly, in the Old Testament, when the Israelites were in foreign lands, part of what made them stand out was their wisdom. Consider, for example, the stories of Joseph (Genesis 41:39; Acts 7:10), Moses (Acts 7:22), Daniel (Daniel 1:20; 5:11), and Ezra (Ezra 7:25). Similarly, in the New Testament, Jesus promised wisdom to his disciples so they could stand up for him (Luke 21:15). Now that we're living in a culture that is increasingly post-Christian, we also can be known for our wisdom.

Our views on ethics have become a barrier to belief in the Christian worldview. Perhaps it's time that our *wisdom* becomes an entry to belief in the Christian worldview. We find wisdom in God's *general* truth, which is available to all. Interestingly, this is exactly what the Old Testament heroes did: Moses learned much wisdom from the Egyptians (Acts 7:22), and Daniel learned wisdom from the Babylonians (Daniel 1:5). Interestingly, Daniel and his friends refused to eat the Babylonian food—that's where they drew the line—but they were happy to learn from their teachers. They went to their schools. They learned their language, culture, and philosophies.

Like Moses and Daniel, we can make a special effort to attend seminars, listen to podcasts, and sign up for courses run by nonbelievers. Not only will this help us find easy common ground with our nonbelieving friends, but it will also open us up to a wider range of God's wisdom. For example, I've learned so much by going to parenting courses run by experts, most of whom are not believers.

I read the *New York Times* and the *New Yorker* regularly. And I have a steady diet of podcasts: *The Moth*, *TED Talks*, *This American Life*, *Conversations* (ABC Radio), *Invisibilia*, *Reply All*, *Pop Culture Happy Hour*, *You Are Not So Smart*, *The Savvy Psychologist*, *Malcolm Gladwell*, *Planet Money*, and *Radio Atlantic*. And at the same time, I have access to God's *special* truth— not only through the Scriptures, but also through the blessings of being a believer—and a Holy Spirit who lives inside me to change me and guide me.

If we put all of this together, we will have a way of life that is obviously *wise* to all. We will stand out—just like Joseph and Daniel stood out in their foreign lands. The evidence will be that our way of life simply works better. Our lifestyle will be attractive (see Titus 2:5, 8, 10).

Just like my friends at the barbecue wanted to talk to me about lawns, our nonbelieving friends will *want* to talk to us about other matters of wisdom. They will ask us for our views.

Wisdom as the Key to Believability

Wisdom provides an entry point into conversations about our faith. But it's more than that. Our wise way of life also makes what we say more believable.

When we in the West were part of a Christianized culture, we used to argue and teach in this sequence: (1) what I say is *true*; (2) if it's true, then you must *believe* it; and (3) if you believe it, you must *live* it.

It's TRUE ⊯ BELIEVE it ⊯ LIVE it

While that may be the correct logical sequence, the way our post-Christian friends discover it is often the reverse sequence: (1) what you see is a wiser way to *live*; (2) but if it's a wiser way to live, then it's also more *believable*; (3) but if it's believable, you need to consider that it might also be *true*.

I can LIVE it → I can BELIEVE it → it must be TRUE

The derogatory expression "How's that working for you?" has become popular recently. It's a great go-to expression when your friend is doing something so unwise it can't possibly be working well for them. For instance, if my friend were to say, "I've been on a strict donut-only diet for the last month," I might be tempted to reply, "So how's that working for you?"

Yet when we do something wise, by and large, it *should* work well for us. Then people will want to listen to us. They will bring up deeper matters and want to hear what we have to say. By being wise, we create opportunities for these conversations. And we will make the Christian worldview more believable.

People Notice

I live on a street where there are a handful of Christian families. These families really are the salt of the earth and the light of the world. They stand out by their kindness, generosity, and hospitality. But they also stand out for their *wisdom*. I know this because one day, one of my non-Christian neighbors said to me, "What is it about you Christians? You just seem to have an extra dose of wisdom about you. You have a way of life that works!" When we're rich in God's wisdom, people notice—and they want to be more like us.

A Chaplain Learns Everybody's Names

I work one or two days a week as an assistant to a variety of orthopedic surgeons. This means I mix regularly with the other surgeons, anesthesiologists, nurses, transporters, and cleaners who work in the surgical suites section of the hospital.

I make a deliberate attempt to learn the names of all the people who work at my section of the hospital—especially the transporters and cleaners. Whenever one of them enters our operating room, I call out their name to make them feel welcome and appreciated.

This is no small thing. I heard from a teacher that one day at his school, a parcel was delivered to someone named Eric. It took a while for people to realize that Eric was the name of the groundskeeper who had been working at the school for twenty years. No one had bothered to learn his name.

Don't just learn the names of those you need to know. Learn the names of the people whose names you *don't* need to know. When you do this, people will realize that you care.

A Chaplain Takes an Interest in People's Lives

My lawyer friend has worked at the same firm for more than ten years. The partners at her firm are always telling her about their vacations and talking about their kids. But they never follow up and ask about hers. Never once have her partners asked her about her vacations. Never once have they asked her about her children or bothered to learn their names. Why? Because they *don't care*!

Don't be like those partners. Show your work friends that you care. Take an interest in their lives by asking what they plan to do on the weekend, what their plans are for summer vacation, and what their children's names are. Write down the names of their partners and children to make sure you don't forget.

Then follow up with some questions to see why these things are important to them. Ask what they like about fishing or what they're looking forward to on their vacation in Europe. Ask why they chose the names they did for their children. Most parents spend a long time choosing a meaningful name for their child, so this is often a fruitful question. Plus, it will make it easier to remember their names.

At my hospital, most of the transporters have tattoos. I love asking them about the meanings of their tattoos, which tattoo they got first, and what tattoo they plan on getting next. Tattoos often have stories attached to them.

The next time you see your friend, follow up with them. Ask them how the fishing trip or the European vacation went. Your work friends will be happy you remembered, and it will show that you cared enough to remember.

The Power of Paying Attention

I am the father of three young boys. A few of the nurses I work with have recently become fathers. To help them through those hard months of parenting infants under the age of three months, I gave each of them my "Daddy Survival Pack"—a bottle of bourbon (I call it the "big brown sleeping pill") and two books on parenting.

One time, I asked one of the nurses if he had drunk the bourbon yet. He exclaimed, "No! I've put the bottle on display. No doctor has ever given me a gift before!"

Look for creative ways to show your coworkers that you have been listening and that you care. It doesn't take much to make a meaningful connection.

A Chaplain Is a Calm, Nonanxious Presence

As a surgical assistant, I often joke that I have the least important job in the operating rooms. The operation could not proceed if any one of the other team members didn't turn up, but it could happily proceed without me.

I said this to one of the nurses one time, and she disagreed. "No! You have the most important job," she said. "You're the one who keeps everybody calm!"

At work, I am apparently the calm, nonanxious presence in my coworker's life. I bring the *shalom* that comes from knowing that God has everything under control. And people notice.

In the parenting seminars I've attended, I've learned

that my role as a parent is also to be the calm, nonanxious presence in my children's lives.[30] What do I mean by *nonanxious*? I mean that we are not anxious about the things we can't control. We calmly submit these to God's power. God has these things under control. If we do this, we will have a calmness about us that we don't even realize. A *shalom*!

A Chaplain Offers to Pray

In medicine, we often joke that you only need to learn to ask two questions to be a psychiatrist. The first is, "How are you doing?" And the second is, "How are you *really* doing?"

According to Genesis 3, every aspect of our human life is cursed. Our work is cursed. Our bodies and health are cursed. Our human relationships are cursed. So all of us are putting on a brave face and pretending that everything is okay when everything can't possibly be okay.

Our job as a de facto chaplain is to invite our friends to share how they are *really* doing at work, health, and home. We become the safe space for them to talk out loud, and then we listen and show that we understand and feel their emotions.

The key is to ask follow-up questions. Just like a psychiatrist, we ask the second question. In fact, I call it *the power of the second question*.

For instance, you may ask, "So how are things at home?" Then you can follow up with, "So . . . how are things at home?" And then pause, showing them that you're inviting them to share how things *really* are at home. This seems simple, but it works. And it provides a great opportunity to offer to pray for someone.

For many weeks, I asked one of the nurses at the hospital, "How are your children—Cassy and Nia?" Every single time she replied, "Good." And that was that. But one day, she replied, "Cassy just saw a child psychologist. She's been a bit slow in some of her development."

Recognizing that this was an invitation to go deeper, I asked her how she felt about that. She said she felt fearful, that she was worried her daughter was going to fall behind. I told her that my wife and I pray every night and asked her if we could pray for her and Cassy.

She replied, "Oh, could you? Yes, that would be wonderful."

Give your friends permission to talk about how things are—*really*. Show them you understand. Acknowledge and affirm their feelings. Offer to pray. Then follow up on it the next time you see them.

Be Jesus

Every morning when I drive my boys to school, we take turns praying for the day ahead. When it's my turn, one of my usual daily prayer requests is, "Heavenly Father, help us to *be Jesus* to those around us today."

Our goal in being a chaplain to those around us is to *be Jesus* to them. Like Jesus, we are the calm, nonanxious presence. We are patient, gentle, gracious, generous, forgiving, and loving. We have wisdom.

Sooner or later, your friend will have a crisis. They will come to you, expecting you to speak on behalf of God. They will ask you to provide meaning and clarity. By coming to you, they are hoping to connect with the transcendent. And they will ask you to perform sacred rituals and prayers.

Bringing Meaning to Tragedy

A boy on our street died suddenly and tragically. It was unbelievably sad, and my family is still saddened by his loss. It united the street in a communal outpouring of grief. But when it came time for the funeral, the parents of the boy asked one of the Christians on our street to preside over the funeral service and give the eulogy. At the service, he spoke on behalf of God. He was our connection with the sacred. His message provided meaning and coherency to a seemingly random and tragic event.

This is exactly what happened to my friend Peter. For years, he and his wife invested time getting to know a family from work. They went to their parties and invited them over for meals. Recently, the family lost a loved one, and they called Peter. They asked him to say some words at the funeral. And they asked him to speak to their grandson over the phone about whether his grandmother was in heaven or hell. This conversation lasted for more than thirty minutes, and other family members listened in. A few weeks after the funeral, Peter and his wife visited the grieving family at their home and provided a meal. Peter became their unofficial, de facto chaplain!

Their Connection with the Sacred

Shawna is an ENT surgeon. At her hospital, there is a transporter named Tatiana. Tatiana is friendly, and everyone else is friendly to her. But Tatiana's body looks older than it should look. It's the kind of body that usually comes from a life of hard living. Tatiana's body is also covered in tattoos, many of which are satanic and pagan symbols.

Shawna learned Tatiana's name. During breaks between operations, Shawna asked Tatiana about her plans for her annual leave. Tatiana excitedly told Shawna she was going to Romania to check out one of her favorite bands.

When Tatiana came back from her vacation, she seemed flat. Shawna asked her about her vacation. Tatiana enthusiastically pulled out her phone and showed Shawna her many vacation photos. Shawna looked at all of them and asked questions to show that she didn't just want to hear what Tatiana was saying; she wanted to feel the same emotions she was feeling.

One night, Shawna and Tatiana happened to be in the dining hall by themselves. Normally the transporters sat by themselves in one corner and the doctors sat by themselves in another corner. But it was just the two of them, so Tatiana got up and sat next to Shawna.

Tatiana shared with Shawna that she used to be a Christian but was badly hurt by the church so she left in disgust. In her anger, she dabbled in satanic music and covered herself in tattoos and satanic symbols. Only in the last few years had Tatiana returned to the Christian faith. She was slowly covering up her old tattoos, one by one. She was slowly fixing up the areas of her life that need fixing up.

That night in the dining hall, Tatiana opened up areas of her life to Shawna that she hadn't revealed to anyone else. Now Shawna prays for Tatiana every day. Shawna has become her unofficial, de facto chaplain. Shawna has become Tatiana's connection with the sacred.

Lean into Disagreement

For Such a Time as This

A while ago, I thought it'd be good to learn how to play chess. That's when I discovered there are three phases to a chess game—the opening or *fore* game, the *middle* game, and the *end* game. In the fore game, you set up your pieces so they're in strong positions. In the middle game, you try to advance your pieces. In the end game, you try to corner your opponent.

It sounded so simple. But I never knew what to do after the first phase—the opening. That's because at that moment, I was as safe as I could possibly be—with all of my pieces set up in front of me. I didn't dare move another piece, to begin the middle game. To do so would automatically open me up and make me vulnerable.

But here's the thing. In order to tell our friends about Jesus, we have to make ourselves vulnerable. Not so much vulnerable to attack, but vulnerable to disagreement. When we do this, we're following in Jesus' footsteps.

Jesus shows us that allowing for disagreement in relationships and being willing to engage with people we disagree with is a way of demonstrating inclusiveness and showing unconditional love. Jesus practiced *inclusion* by eating and drinking with those who disagreed with him. When we make room for disagreement, we also show that we value inclusiveness. After all, if we only eat with those who agree with us, we're practicing exclusion by turning away those who disagree with us.

Jesus also demonstrated *unconditional love* by telling his followers to love and bless those who disagreed with them. When we engage with people we disagree with, we also demonstrate unconditional love. You see, if we only love those who agree with us, that's conditional love, not unconditional.

If we believe in true inclusion and unconditional love, we have to be able to disagree with each other.

The Gospel Will Be Necessarily Offensive

Sooner or later, we *have* to disagree. Every culture will eventually find something it disagrees with about the gospel. For the Athenians, it was that there was such a thing as a resurrection (Acts 17:32). For Nicodemus, it was that you had to be born again (John 3:3–4). For the woman at the well, it was that the Jews taught that worship had to take place in Jerusalem (John 4:20).

Probably none of those things would be offensive to our post-Christian Western culture today. But we've found other things about the gospel that we think are offensive. For instance, Western culture dislikes the idea that people need saving, that there is such a thing as evil, that there is such a destination as hell for the unsaved, that God has a right to tell us how to live, that God needs to punish sins, that God's salvation is exclusive. Western culture particularly dislikes the Bible's views on sex and morality.

What is necessarily offensive for one culture is not necessarily offensive for another culture. Culture determines what we do or don't find offensive about the gospel.

This doesn't mean we must try to make our message offensive. It also doesn't mean that unless we've been offensive, we haven't communicated the gospel. We can't control how a person responds. But it does mean that sooner or later our friend will find something they disagree with about the gospel. This is exactly why we were told *not* to talk about religion and politics at the dinner table.

But now we've done it. We've gone ahead and told our friend about Jesus—which is the whole purpose of this book. Now what? How do we disagree, and how do we do it well?

Our View Is Jesus' View

When it comes to points that our friends will disagree with, I like to say that I hold the same views Jesus holds. The advantage of this approach is that post-Christian society views authority figures—such as the church—as *oppressive* because they impose their versions of salvation on us. But for some reason, our Western culture does not lump Jesus in the same category as the institutionalized church. Instead, our culture views Jesus himself as some sort of subversive, countercultural hero.

Another advantage of this approach is that it places the basis of our belief on Jesus. We don't believe what we believe because this is what we *prefer to be true*; we believe what we believe because this is what Jesus himself tells us *is true*.

So if my friend asks me to explain how a loving God can send people to hell, I point them to Jesus' parable of the rich man and Lazarus (Luke 16:19–31). I ask them to read it with me, and then I ask them to tell me what they like about this story and to tell me what it says about hell. The interesting thing is that in the *context of the story*, hell makes perfect sense—of course the rich man should be in hell, while Lazarus should be in heaven. Most of our post-Christian friends would agree. This fits their idea of justice. But more importantly, it shows that we believe in hell, not because we *prefer* to believe in hell, but because Jesus teaches us that hell exists.

Or when my friend asks me about my views on same-sex marriage—another topic pretty much guaranteed to be divisive—I can reply that I have the same view as Jesus. When it comes to issues of sex and morality, we all believe that some forms of sex are good, but there are other forms of sex that are wrong. In other words, we all have sexual *norms*. But the basis for our norms might differ. As followers of Jesus, we believe that Jesus is the basis for our norms. Jesus is the one who made us and loves us, and he gets to tell us what to do. When it comes to same-sex marriage, if we're disagreeing, it's not over issues of love, inclusion, or human rights. If we're disagreeing, it's over what Jesus tells us is right or wrong. Again, this shows that my views on sex and morality are not centered around what I *prefer* to be moral or immoral, but around what Jesus teaches me is moral or immoral.

Using Stories to Answer Questions

Sharing stories to answer questions is great because no one can argue against a story. One question my nonbelieving friends often ask is, "What about those who haven't heard about Jesus?" I usually tell them about my friend Michael, who had grown up in Iran, which was closed to Christianity. He had no access to the Bible, churches, or the Christian message. But one night, Jesus came to Michael in a dream, and ever since that day, Michael has believed in Jesus. Or I tell them about Sharon, who was living in China when Jesus appeared to her in a dream. She subsequently became a Christian, started going to church, and gained access to the Bible.

These stories show that God finds creative ways to make himself known, especially to those without access to the Bible. But according to Jesus, the Bible is the clearest message about God that there is (Luke 16:31). So for those of us with access to the Bible, God doesn't have to find these creative ways. After all, we've got the Bible!

Another question my friends often ask is, "Doesn't religion cause hatred and violence?" I share the story of when I was at St James Church in Kenilworth, Cape Town, South Africa. Inside the church, I saw the bullet holes in the wall from when gunmen stormed into the church during a Sunday worship service and sprayed bullets into the congregation, killing eleven worshipers and wounding fifty-eight. Remarkably the church publicly forgave the gunmen. My story helpfully provides the counterargument that Jesus' teachings will have the opposite effect of violence. Jesus teaches us to love our enemies and to be peacemakers.

Or I could share the biblical story of Peter, who pulled out a sword to cut off the ear of the servant sent to arrest Jesus. But Jesus heals the servant's ear and tells Peter to put away his sword (John 18:10–11). This story clearly teaches that Jesus wants his followers to avoid violence. How can you argue against a story like that?

Gently Challenge Their Worldview

I once heard a bivocational Christian pastor say that when he was in his secular work, he was constantly being bombarded with questions. He answered these questions as best he could in order to explain the Christian faith, but eventually he grew tired of always being on the defensive. So one day he switched it around. He started asking his work friends questions. Suddenly they were the ones having to defend and explain their positions.

Everyone is only two "why" questions away from not being able to give a rational answer. If we start asking questions, our nonbelieving friends will realize that much of their worldview is based not on rational arguments or evidence but on brute-force statements that they believe at face value without evidence.

In the Bible, Jesus often doesn't answer the questions people ask him. Instead, he asks a question in return. For instance, when asked to give his views on taxes, he responds, "Show me a denarius. Whose image and inscription are on it?" (Luke 20:24). Or when Jesus is asked where he gets his authority, he says, "I will also ask you a question. Tell me: John's baptism—was it from heaven, or of human origin?" (Luke 20:3–4).

The topics that lead to fruitful discussions are human rights and dignity, equality, and freedom. Let's explore each of these topics further. Here are a few questions we can ask.

Where do you get your views on human rights and dignity? As a Christian, I derive my views on human rights and dignity from our being created in the image of God. Or I can point to Christ's incarnation—the Son of God became one of us. Or I can appeal to Jesus, who said, "Whatever you did for one of the least of these brothers and sisters of mine, you did for me" (Matthew 25:40).

But if I don't hold the Christian worldview, where can I derive my views on human rights and dignity from? All I can do is cling to human laws and conventions. But these are arbitrary social constructs—and they are *Western* social constructs. So if I speak of human rights and dignity from this basis, I'm actually guilty of imposing my Western values on other cultures that don't hold similar views. Without a God who transcends human conventions, the belief in universal human rights and dignity will be reduced to another form of Western imperialism.

Where do you get your views on human equality? In our Western culture today, we champion the weak, the poor, and the marginalized. But why? Where did this notion come from?

As a Christian, I can appeal to how the God of the Bible is the champion of the underdog—Abel over Cain, Sarah over Hagar, Jacob over Esau, Leah over Rachel, Israel over the nations. I can point out how Jesus hung out with the marginalized and how Jesus, the Son of God, lowered himself and became a slave who died an outcast's death on a cross (Philippians 2:5–8).

But if I don't have this Christian worldview, how can I defend my views on human equality? I can't appeal to Mother Nature or to the animal kingdom. Animal behavior and society are brutally hierarchical. I can't appeal to this being hardwired into us as part of our evolutionary instincts. Because even if this was true in the past, why *should* it continue to be true for me, the individual, in the present? Moreover, our ideas of human equality are very *Western*. If I impose these views, I'm again guilty of promoting Western cultural superiority.

Why do you believe in human freedom? Freedom is the chief idol of the West. It's enshrined in the national anthems of many Western countries, including France, the United States, Australia, and Canada. It's found in the United States Declaration of Independence. It's in the French Revolution's motto *"Liberté, Egalité, Fraternité"* ("Liberty, Equality, Fraternity"). But where did we get the idea that humans ought to be free?

As a Christian, I can appeal to God, who created freely and gave human beings choices, responsibilities, and free will. I can point out that the word *free* (or related words) appears almost two hundred times in the Bible. I can appeal to Jesus Christ, who comes to set us free (Luke 4:18; John 8:32). Indeed, the Bible associates salvation with freedom (Romans 6:7).[31]

But what is freedom if I don't believe in God? If we are only physical atoms and molecules, then we can only be living in a mechanical universe of cause and effect. This is a universe of *determinism*, where freedom is only an illusion. The atheist philosopher Yuval Noah Harari argues that notions such as freedom are merely useful fictional stories we've been telling ourselves.[32] Yet we hold people accountable for their choices. Consider the recent #MeToo movement and today's call-out culture. The very premise of these movements is that humans do indeed have freedom and can make morally accountable choices. But where does this freedom come from if there's no God?

We talk about freedom as freedom *from* constraints. That is to say, we ought to be free from what we're told by society, tradition, our families, or religion. But without God, once these constraints are removed, we have no idea what we're free *for*. What exactly are we supposed to do with our freedom? We are rudderless. We have no direction. This is because we actually don't know *why* we're here on this planet. If there is no God and we are here by random, blind chance, then any talk of purpose is meaningless. And, worse, if we don't have to be here, it's only a small leap to start talking about how we *shouldn't* be here. We're only in the way of other, more important life forms.

So what are we free *for*? To answer this requires knowing our purpose. But any talk of purpose requires knowing our design. A watch's purpose is to tell time—that is what it's designed for. A pen's purpose is to write—that is what it's designed for. A lamp's purpose is to give light—that is what it's designed for. If we are to have any sense of our purpose as humans, we need to know what we were designed for. To do so requires knowing our Designer. This is why Jesus claims to give us freedom (John 8:32). We will not only be set free *from* constraints, but we will also know what we're set free *for*. If we know Jesus, we will know our Designer. And our chief purpose is to be fulfilled in Jesus.

Our friend may reply that they can create their own purpose. But trying to create our own purpose is like a nation that prints its own money. You can't generate wealth just by printing money. The money by itself has no value unless it's linked to an external reference point. In the same way, we can't create our own purpose. We can try, but ultimately it will be valueless unless we can link it to an external reference point—God's purpose for us.

Practicing Positive Apologetics

In the past, there was a lot of talk about *defeater beliefs*— i.e., beliefs that our nonbelieving friends have that supposedly *defeat* our Christian beliefs. Here are some of the usual culprits in our post-Christian Western culture:

- How can you trust the Bible?
- What about other religions?
- Why can't God just forgive?

- What are your views on sex and morality?
- How can God allow suffering?
- Aren't Christians just hypocrites?
- Hasn't science disproved the Bible?

These defeater beliefs are very specific to a culture. For example, if you were in Taiwan, the defeater belief might be, "But what about my parents? I can't change religions because this will cause them too much public shame and grief." Or if you were in a more Christianized culture, the defeater belief might be, "I've gone to church all my life; that's enough to get me into heaven."

I believe that all Christians should be aware of what defeater beliefs our friends might have in their particular culture—and figure out some ways to respond to these defeater beliefs.[33] One strategy is to let our friends know how culturally specific their objections are. If our friend lived in another time or place, they wouldn't have those objections. Their current objections are determined by their culture.

In the last five to ten years, I believe our culture has become even more post-Christian, to the extent that the common defeater beliefs we listed above may not even be an issue. Our friends aren't nonbelievers because the defeater beliefs on that list are stopping them from believing; our friends are nonbelievers because they don't even know why they need to believe in the Christian God of the Bible.

We need to move beyond responding to defeater beliefs (practicing *negative* apologetics). Instead, we need to give reasons that promote belief (practicing *positive* apologetics).

We need to show our nonbelieving friends why they *need* or *want* Christianity to be true.

Let's say you and your non-Christian friend are discussing marriage. You agree that a husband ought to love his wife and not treat her as mere property. You disagree about needing the God of the Bible for this to be true. Challenge your friend to prove, based on any other reason, that a husband ought to love his wife. Your friend will try. They'll give reasons like, "It's a good thing to do"; "It's the right thing to do"; or "A woman has dignity." But that's simply question-begging. Your friend is merely repeating the conclusion in different words. But so far, your friend still hasn't given a reason why a husband *ought* to love his wife.

Or let's say you and your friend are discussing human rights. You and your friend agree that there's such a thing as universal human rights—that things like slavery and the sex trade are wrong. You disagree about needing the God of the Bible for this to be true. Challenge your friend to prove, based on any other reason, that a human being has an inherent dignity, value, or worth apart from what they achieve or acquire in this life. Again, they may try to give reasons—appealing, for example, to the United Nations Universal Declaration of Human Rights—but these are all arbitrary human social conventions. And not all cultures and nations hold these to be true. This allows you to point out that unless there's a God who created us as inherently worthy—in his image—and confers dignity on us by becoming one of us and dying for us, it's very hard to believe in such a thing as human rights. You can also point out that this is unique to the Judeo-Christian worldview. I'm not sure whether there is any other religious worldview in which God or the gods value the life of each and every human. In fact, it's quite the contrary. In most other religions, the gods don't care about the humans. At best, the gods might be coerced into being merciful to the humans every now and then, but at worst, the gods see the human race as an inconvenience.

As another example, I like to say we want to believe that God is a loving God. In fact, this is the starting premise to most of the *objections* against the Christian worldview. For example, "How can a loving God allow suffering?" Or, "How can a loving God send people to hell?" Or, "How can a loving God not accept me for who I am?" But I like to ask gently, "Where do we get the idea that God needs to be loving?" We actually only get it from the Judeo-Christian worldview. In no other religion is God obligated to be loving. In fact, again, it's quite the contrary. In other religions, the gods are simply uncaring. Or worse, they can be mischievous, malicious, or capricious—working against our best intentions rather than with them. So if we want to hold to the premise that God is obligated to be loving, then we actually also need the God of the Bible to be true.

Tim Keller's book *Making Sense of God* uses a similar approach to what we're doing here. Whereas his *Reason for God* was focused on addressing defeater beliefs, *Making Sense of God* is focused on promoting reasons why we need to believe in the existence of God.[34] In this book, Keller shows how much of what we believe to be true—e.g., meaning, satisfaction, freedom, self, identity, hope, morality, and justice—are nonsensical unless the God of the Bible is also true. They cannot exist without a transcendent God who made us, loves us, and saves us. I believe we can use this approach in the art of *positive* apologetics.[35]

Win the Friendship, Not the Argument

This whole chapter may give you the wrong impression—that it's all about winning the argument. You may be thinking that all we need is a great sound bite, a gotcha moment, a meme, a clever presentation of evidence, a smart turn of phrase, or a logical reason. All these things are useful and important, but they almost never make someone change their beliefs.

That's because no one ever wants to lose an argument. We have a very strong aversion to loss.[36] So our friends will rarely change their beliefs if it means they've lost an argument. They would prefer to double down on their original belief than admit to losing. They will engage in what psychologists call confirmation bias, post hoc reasoning, and motivated reasoning—all to stop them from having to change their beliefs.

Instead, we can show them that it's not "us versus them." It's not "I'm right, and you're wrong." Instead, we're both after the same thing—we're just coming from different starting points. So if they change their beliefs, they're not *losing* the argument; instead, they are changing beliefs because they are seeing things from a *new perspective*.[37]

We arrive at this new perspective by asking these sorts of questions:[38]

- **What is it that you want?** Here they can describe what they're looking for.
- **Why is this important to you?** This reveals the deeper issue that's driving them.
- **Why do you think we see things differently?** This helps them see things from our point of view (often for the first time ever). They now have to stand in our shoes and empathize with us.
- **What would it take for you to trust me? Or Jesus? Or the Bible?** This reveals the real roadblock standing in their way of believing in the gospel, and it helps us see if there's anything we can lovingly do to remove that obstacle.

Here's an example of how the conversation could go:

What is it that you want?

I'm for marriage equality.

Why is this important to you?

I believe in human dignity and justice.

Why do you think we see things differently?

131

I don't believe in a God. I believe we're just atoms and molecules and another species of life on this planet. I believe we only live once, so we've got to do what makes us happy in this life—and no one has the right to tell anyone else what to do.

But you believe there's a God. You believe you are more than the sum of your parts. You believe it's God who confers dignity on every human. You believe God is the basis of justice. And you believe God has the right to tell us what to do because he loves us and made us. So we're both after the same things—human dignity and justice. It's just that you believe we need God for those things, and I don't.

Up until now I thought you were against marriage equality because you were a religious jerk who was against human dignity and justice. Now I can see that it's simply because you believe there's a God who makes the rules and not us. I don't agree with you, but I can see your point of view—for the first time.

What would it take for you to trust the Bible?

I don't think I ever could. I feel so betrayed by the church. When my mother was divorced by my father, her church shunned and shamed her. I'll never forgive the church for that. I need someone to apologize for what they did before I could start to listen.

In this example, our friend's nonbelief isn't because they can't trust the Bible's historical accuracy; it's really because they've been hurt by the church. But if we hadn't asked this question, we would have been presenting all sorts of arguments that weren't addressing the real need—i.e., the church's need to apologize to our friend and their mother. Now that we know the true roadblock to our friend's belief, we can go about dealing with it lovingly.

For Such a Time as This

The problem Christianity had during the age of Christendom was that we confused our Western culture with Christianity, as if they were the same thing. The beautiful thing in our post-Christian age is that the gospel is wonderfully foreign again. The gospel is foreign to any and every culture. This is its strength rather than its weakness.

In much of the Bible, we see God's people working out how to be foreigners in a foreign land. In the Old Testament, we have Joseph, Moses, Daniel, Esther, Ezra, Nehemiah, and Jonah, among others. And in the New Testament, we have Peter in Caesarea and Paul on his missionary journeys—particularly before foreign powers (e.g., Agrippa) and audiences (e.g., the Areopagus in Athens). It seems that a key part of our identity as God's people is knowing how to be foreigners (1 Peter 1:1).

Interestingly, part of being a foreigner is also knowing how to speak up when we must. On the one hand, this isn't easy. Moses worried that he wasn't gifted enough to speak (Exodus 4:10). Nehemiah was afraid of the king's anger (Nehemiah 2:1–3). Esther feared for her life (Esther 4:11). On the other hand, this is often exactly why God has placed us in these situations—so we can speak up. Mordecai's words to Esther may also be for us: "Who knows but that you have come to your royal position for such a time as this?" (Esther 4:14).

Perhaps "for such a time as this" can be our motto. We live in interesting times. Our friends are more skeptical than ever. In much of the Western world, we are now post-Christian, post-churched, post-reached, and post-millennial. But these are also exciting times. Jesus promised his followers that one day we would have to speak up for him (Luke 21:12–13). What we may think of as threats to our witness are actually God-given opportunities to speak on his behalf.

Conclusion: Looking for Black Swan Moments

Evangelism Happens When We Least Expect It

In 2007, Nassim Nicholas Taleb wrote the groundbreaking book *The Black Swan*, which spent almost a year on the *New York Times* bestseller list. In this book, Taleb argues that many momentous events are outliers that people could not have predicted. These events occur tangentially and were not even what the discoverers were looking for in the first place.

For example, Dr Alexander Fleming's discovery of penicillin was a random accident, when he found that the mold on his Petri dish unexpectedly killed bacteria.[39] Taleb's book concludes that we should embrace the seemingly randomness of life's events and just go out there and see what happens. We won't find what we're looking for, but something else that we're not looking for will find us.

Much of evangelism occurs the same way. Often we go out looking for opportunities to evangelize, but they just don't happen. Instead, we should just go out there *and be Jesus to the community*—and the opportunities to evangelize will find us.

135

A few years ago, my wife, Steph, was in a busy shopping mall with our three young boys—at that time ages three, five, and seven. The mall was crowded. The boys were tired and hungry after the school day. But Steph noticed a young Asian woman holding her baby daughter and looking extremely distressed. Steph learned that the woman's name was Jenna, and she asked her if everything was okay. Jenna replied that she couldn't find her elderly mother, who was not able to speak English and who had the baby carriage—along with Jenna's purse, money, mobile phone, and food for the baby.

Steph spent the next few hours helping Jenna look for her mother. They walked up and down the mall, visited shops outside the mall, and even called the police to report her mother as missing. Steph offered food to Jenna so she could feed her hungry baby. Finally they found her mother.

Jenna thanked Steph profusely for her time, and Steph seized the opportunity to invite Jenna to the playgroup at our church. From there we invited Jenna to come to our church. When Jenna's husband, Nelson, saw all the happy families worshiping at the church, he said to Jenna, "Whatever these people believe, we have to believe the same thing!"

We invited Jenna to come to our adult small group, which meets at our home for lunch after our Sunday church service. That day we had a large barbecue. Jenna was intrigued. Being a new immigrant to Australia, she also wanted to learn how to host a barbecue at her own place. So we offered to help her and supplied her with our grill.

Jenna hosted a barbecue at her place. She invited

families from our church's playgroup and families from a different (non-church) playgroup that she also attended, where most of the families were nonbelievers. The two groups mingled. Many nonbelievers met believers at the barbecue, chatted, and formed new friendships.

One of the non-Christian couples we met there has become our friends and are now attending a local church with another Christian couple they met at Jenna's barbecue.

Shortly after Jenna's barbecue, one of the couples suffered a tragedy—the husband was injured in a motorbike accident and became a quadriplegic. The couple met our church's pastor, who was also in a motorcycle accident and is now himself a quadriplegic. The wife has started coming to my wife's midweek Bible study group with other mothers.

Can you see what happened? At least three couples are now checking out Jesus because my wife, Steph, stopped to help Jenna at a shopping mall a few years ago. This wasn't what Steph had in mind at the time. Back then, she was just going out of her way to help a distressed shopper. She was *being Jesus* to the other woman. But that one act triggered a set of unforeseen, tangential sequences of events that resulted in evangelism. This is exactly what Nassim Nicholas Taleb would call a "black swan" moment.

Maybe we can do the same thing. In addition to our deliberate efforts to *do evangelism*—to create opportunities for evangelism—we just need to *be Jesus*, and evangelism opportunities may well come and find us in unforeseen and exciting ways.

Other Resources

Using Stories to Tell the Gospel

Chan, Sam, *Evangelism in a Skeptical World: How to Make the Unbelievable News about Jesus More Believable.* Grand Rapids: Zondervan, 2018. Especially chapter 7.

Dillon, Christine, *Telling the Gospel Through Story: Evangelism That Keeps Hearers Wanting More.* Downers Grove, IL: InterVarsity, 2012.

International Orality Network (ION), orality.net.

Storying the Scriptures: Telling the Gospel through Story, www.storyingthescriptures.com.

Wycliffe Bible Translators: *Story the Bible* workshops, https://wycliffe.org.au/eventtype/story-the-bible-workshop.

Becoming a Bible Page-Turner

The Word One to One, www.theword121.com; publisher: 10 Publishing, www.10ofthose.com.

Workplace Evangelism

I work for City Bible Forum, which promotes ways for people to tell their coworkers about Jesus. The pamphlet below, which we give to Christian workers, contains many of the principles found in this book.

COFFEE

Coffee is an easy invite. It's only ten minutes. You'll be in a "public" space. And the conversation will be about "safe" topics, such as the weather, sports, and movies.

- Ask what they're listening to or watching.
- Ask what they plan to do on the weekend.
- Ask about their family.

Listen properly! Learn the names of their children, spouses, hobbies, TV shows, vacation spots.

And here's the key:

The next time you meet for coffee, ask follow-up questions from last time.

- How is Brianna doing at school?

- How was the picnic with your old school friend?
- How many episodes did you get to watch on Netflix?
- What do you enjoy about cooking?

DINNER

Dinner (or lunch) is a "bigger" invite. Now we're looking at investing sixty minutes. You'll be in a "private" space. Here the conversation will move to "values" and "worldviews."

Ask questions that allow them to safely talk about issues close to them:

- How are things at home?
- How are things at work?
- How are things with your parents?
- How are things with the neighbors?

Our job is simply to listen and to understand where they're coming from.

Then ask questions that give them permission to open up:

- How do you feel about that?
- How do you think that's going?
- What are you going to do?

GOSPEL

Sooner or later, we have the permission to start "sacred" conversations.

Ask questions such as:

- What religion did your parents have? What was that like?
- Do you have a faith? Tell me about it.
- Do you pray? Tell me about it.

They may ask you the same questions in return!

Bit by bit, we can become the de facto chaplain in their life. And bit by bit, they will come and ask us to share more and more about our faith. This is where we can share:

- how we became a Christian
- how God works in our life
- a story about Jesus from the Bible
- our favorite gospel outline

Tell them you'll pray for them, and follow up on this the next time you meet.

NEXT STEPS

Contact City Bible Forum to get:

- free resources such as *The Word One to One*
- Sam's book *Evangelism in a Skeptical World* for his favorite gospel outline

Evangelism works better in a team rather than solo.

Contact City Bible Forum to be connected with other Christians in your workplace.

Acknowledgments

I can't dance. That's why I didn't dance at my own wedding. Why would I want to publicly humiliate myself in front of friends and family? I also can't sing. That's why you won't find any of my songs on Spotify or YouTube.

But I'm also not a writer. I was a science and math geek in high school. English literature was my least favorite subject. I much preferred balancing a chemical equation to writing an essay. If you told me back then that I would be writing books for an international audience, I would have told you you've confused me for some other Asian author called "Chan"—maybe Francis Chan?

But this all changed a few years ago. A bunch of my Aussie buddies—Kit Barker, Malcolm Gill, Alan Thompson, Kirk Patston, Ian Maddock—felt sorry for me during a wilderness period of my life. They cheered me up by taking me along with them to a nerdy theology conference (ETS) in the USA. It was here that they inspired me to become a writer.

But a writer needs a publisher. At ETS, I pitched my book idea to Zondervan. But as an unknown Aussie writer, I had a very slim chance—or as we say in Australia, "a Buckley's chance"—of success. But Ryan Pazdur and Joshua Kessler from Zondervan took a chance on me (maybe they confused me with Francis Chan?), and for that I'll always be grateful.

But a writer also needs editors. At heart, I'm still a science and math geek. I can write a string of quadratic equations but not a string of smooth English sentences. If this book reads well—and it does!—it's because of a skilled team of editors, including Ryan Pazdur, Elizabeth Vince, and Dirk Buursma. Yes, it took a team of at least three editors to transform my incoherent gobbledygook into this easy-to-read book.

But a writer also needs to be set free. This is where I'll forever be thankful to my employer, City Bible Forum, in Australia. My bosses—Al Stewart, Mark Leong, Peter Kaldor—are at the same time humble and secure. They celebrate the successes of others instead of being threatened by them. They give me permission to explore fresh ideas, and they give me the freedom to fail. They work for the kingdom and not their own personal towers of Babel.

City Bible Forum has a team of highly gifted evangelists—Caroline Spencer, Grace Huang, Jessica Halim, Sharon Cheung, Craig Josling, Russ Matthews, Stephen McAlpine, David Robertson, Andrew Laird, David Chan (yes, another Chan!), Rob Martin, Barry Allan, Kim Riley, Peter Wrench, David Pitt, Scott Paisley, Martin Chung, Leon Hribar, Leni McMillan, Lachlan Orr, Ken West, Derek McComber, Aaron Johnstone, Wilbur Longbottom (I think he'd prefer Chan as a surname)—just to name a few. I wish I could list the whole team, but that would take another book. These people are the real thing. They are legit. If I said anything original in this book, it's because I learned it from these people first. They are front-line evangelists with years of experience in our new post-Christendom world. Check out their blogs and podcasts at *plus.citybibleforum.org*.

But a writer also needs a solid home base. The journey of writing a book is an emotional roller coaster, with super high highs and depressingly low lows. My writings would be impossible without my wife, Stephanie. She is my biggest cheerleader . . . even though she's yet to finish one of my books. (Hint: if you've made it past chapter 2 of my previous award-winning book, *Evangelism in a Skeptical World*, then you've already read more of that book than she has.)

Thanks also to my three boys—Toby, Cooper, and Jonty—who are my emotional compass. They teach me not to take life too seriously. Everything can be solved by "outdoor time"—climbing trees, backyard cricket, and kicking the footy.

But, finally, a writer needs a journey. I have been profoundly shaped by my PhD journey, which took me to Trinity Evangelical Divinity School (TEDS), Deerfield, Illinois. My five years in Chicago shaped me into the person I am now. But this journey was *only possible* because of the generous support of my parents, Winnie and Joseph. This book is a legacy of their belief in me.

Notes

1. Sam Chan, *Evangelism in a Skeptical World: How to Make the Unbelievable News about Jesus More Believable* (Grand Rapids: Zondervan, 2018).
2. If someone you know complains that this book is not sufficiently theologically nerdy for them, tell them to read my earlier book. There's enough theological talk there to keep them happy for a long time.
3. See Alex Williams, "Why Is It Hard to Make Friends Over 30?" *New York Times*, July 13, 2012, www.nytimes.com /2012/07/15/fashion/the-challenge-of-making-friends-as-an -adult.html. Atul Gawande also observes that the quality of friendships increases in the later years of life (*Being Mortal: Medicine and What Matters in the End* [New York: Metropolitan, 2014], 97–98).
4. See Sebastian Junger, *Tribe: On Homecoming and Belonging* (New York: Hachette, 2016).
5. David McRaney, "The Life-Threatening Impact of Loneliness and How to Combat It in Our Modern, Insular World" (Episode 139), *You Are Not So Smart*, November 21, 2018, https://youarenotsosmart.com/2018/11/21/yanss-139-the-life -threatening-impact-of-loneliness-and-how-to-combat-it-in-our -modern-insular-world; see also Kate Leaver, *The Friendship Cure: Reconnecting the Modern World* (New York: Abrams, 2019); Shankar Vedantam, Rhaina Cohen, and Tara Boyle, "Guys, We Have a Problem: How American Masculinity

Creates Lonely Men," *Hidden Brain*, October 14, 2019, www
.npr.org/2019/10/11/769538697/guys-we-have-a-problem-how
-american-masculinity-creates-lonely-men. I owe this reference
to David Owen and Hunter Young from Providence Baptist
Church, Raleigh, North Carolina.

6. See George Monbiot, "The Age of Loneliness Is Killing Us,"
The Guardian, October 14, 2014, www.theguardian.com
/commentisfree/2014/oct/14/age-of-loneliness-killing-us.

7. See Katherine Gillespie, "Loneliness Survey Finds
Australians Are Very, Very Lonely," *VICE*, September 26,
2016, www.vice.com/en_au/article/5ge5v3/loneliness-survey
-finds-that-australians-are-very-lonely.

8. See Jon Ronson, *So You've Been Publicly Shamed* (New York:
Riverhead, 2016).

9. See David McRaney, "How Our Unchecked Tribal Psychology
Pollutes Politics, Science, and Just about Everything Else"
(Episode 122), *You Are Not So Smart*, February 26, 2018,
https://youarenotsosmart.com/2018/02/26/yanss-122-how-our
-unchecked-tribal-psychology-pollutes-politics-science-and
-just-about-everything-else.

10. See David McRaney, "The Backfire Effect–Part Four"
(Episode 144), *You Are Not So Smart*, January 19, 2019,
https://youarenotsosmart.com/2019/01/19/yanss-144-the
-backfire-effect-part-four.

11. I'm benefiting from Greg Lukianoff and Jonathan Haidt's
insights in *The Coddling of the American Mind: How Good
Intentions and Bad Ideas Are Setting Up a Generation for
Failure* (New York: Penguin, 2019), 263, where they quote
Aleksandr Solzhenitsyn: "The line dividing good and evil cuts
through the heart of every human being."

12. Nathan Campbell, "Evangelism as Team Sport (A Review of
Sam Chan's *Evangelism in a Skeptical World*)," St. Eutychus,
https://st-eutychus.com/2018/evangelism-as-team-sport-a
-review-of-sam-chans-evangelism-in-a-skeptical-world.

13. I owe the observations here to Pete Ritchie, the ministry team leader of FOCUS, a ministry to the military in Australia (www.focusmilitary.org.au).

14. I learned this particular question from Wendy Potts and Stephen Dinning, who are gifted evangelists in the Wollongong area of Sydney.

15. CRU Camps is a division of Crusader Union of Australia, which runs Christian camps for children and teens.

16. I love this one. Once again, to be clear, I learned this particular question from Wendy Potts and Stephen Dinning.

17. James Veltmeyer taught me about this particular question —i.e., "What's the *best* thing about _____?"

18. If you want to explore the "science" behind hospitality, Nathan Campbell has alerted me to a fascinating essay by Mary Douglas titled "Deciphering a Meal," in *Implicit Meanings* (New York: Routledge, 1999), 231-51, http://chnm.gmu.edu /courses/omalley/610/douglas.pdf.

19. Elmer John Thiessen, *The Scandal of Evangelism: A Biblical Study of the Ethics of Evangelism* (Eugene, OR: Cascade, 2018), 115.

20. See Jade Wu, "4 Secrets Therapists Use to Be a Great Listener," *Savvy Psychologist* (Episode 257), Quick and Dirty Tips, August 30, 2019, www.quickanddirtytips.com/relationships/friendships/ secrets-good-listener; see also Ellen Hendriksen, "How to Be an Amazing Listener," *Savvy Psychologist* (Episode 163), Quick and Dirty Tips, July 28, 2017, www.quickanddirtytips.com /relationships/etiquette-manners/how-to-be-an-amazing-listener.

21. I owe much of the observations on this point to Andrew Katay, who is an Anglican minister in Sydney, Australia.

22. I'm borrowing this title from UK Christian psychiatrist Glynn Harrison's book, *A Better Story: God, Sex & Human Flourishing* (London: Inter-Varsity, 2016).

23. See my previous book, *Evangelism in a Skeptical World: How to Make the Unbelievable News about Jesus More Believable*

(Grand Rapids: Zondervan, 2018), for additional possible factors (see especially the discussions on pages 169–70 and 283).

24. Superb treatments of secularism as a story line can be found in Mark Sayers's excellent podcast series *This Cultural Moment*, especially "What Is Deconstructionism? The Secular Salvation Schema" (season 3, episode 4), November 27, 2018, https://thisculturalmoment.podbean.com/e/the-secular-salvation-schema.

25. Shared by Tim Keller in "Dwelling in the Gospel," NYC Dwell Conference, April 30, 2008, https://vimeo.com/channels/331640/8977644; see also "Dwelling in the Gospel by Dr. Tim Keller," LifeCoach4God, July 30, 2012, https://lifecoach4god.life/2012/07/30/dwelling-in-the-gospel-by-dr-tim-keller.

26. Once again, I learned this great question from my friend James Veltmeyer.

27. I owe this insight to Caroline Spencer, who is my colleague at City Bible Forum.

28. These, of course, are the questions used in the storytelling method—which you can explore further in my *Evangelism in a Skeptical World*, p. 181; see Christine Dillon, *Telling the Gospel through Story: Evangelism That Keeps Hearers Wanting More* (Downers Grove, IL: InterVarsity, 2012). For more information, check out Christine Dillon's website (storyingthescriptures.com) and the International Orality Network (ION) website (orality.net), or enroll in a Wycliffe Bible Storytelling Workshop.

29. Australian chaplain Warren Crank has written an excellent book on how to do this; see *Unofficial Chaplain: A Handbook for Everyday Service to the People around You* (Brisbane: CHI-Books, 2017).

30. By this I don't mean we can't struggle with *clinical* or *medical* anxiety. I recognize that many Christians struggle with anxiety, just as many Christians struggle with physical illnesses.

Notes

31. Timothy Keller frames Christian salvation as freedom in *The Freedom of Self-Forgetfulness: The Path to True Christian Joy* (Farington, Leyland, UK: 10Publishing, 2012); see also Abdu Murray, *Saving Truth: Finding Meaning and Clarity in a Post-Truth World* (Grand Rapids: Zondervan, 2018), 71–92. For an extensive treatment on freedom, see Os Guinness, *Last Call for Liberty: How America's Genius for Freedom Has Become Its Greatest Threat* (Downers Grove, IL: InterVarsity, 2018).

32. See Yuval Noah Harari, "The Myth of Freedom," *The Guardian*, September 14, 2018, www.theguardian.com/books /2018/sep/14/yuval-noah-harari-the-new-threat-to-liberal -democracy.

33. Timothy Keller's *The Reason for God: Belief in an Age of Skepticism* (New York: Penguin, 2009) is an excellent resource for responding to these defeater beliefs.

34. Tim Keller, *Making Sense of God: An Invitation to the Skeptical* (New York: Viking, 2016).

35. See Sarah Eekhoff Zylstra, "Ask and You Shall Evangelize," Gospel Coalition, November 14, 2018, www.thegospelcoalition .org/article/ask-shall-evangelize.

36. See Daniel Kahneman, *Thinking, Fast and Slow* (New York: Farrar, Straus and Giroux, 2011), 283–304.

37. See David McRaney, "How to Talk to People about Things," *You Are Not So Smart* (Episode 143), December 17, 2018, https://youarenotsosmart.com/2018/12/17/yanss-143-how-to -talk-to-people-about-things.

38. I appropriated these questions from Misha Glouberman in his interview with David McRaney, "How to Talk to People about Things."

39. Nassim Nicholas Taleb, *The Black Swan: The Impact of the Highly Improbable* (New York: Random House, 2007), 167.

Evangelism in a Skeptical World

How to Make the Unbelievable News about Jesus More Believable

Sam Chan

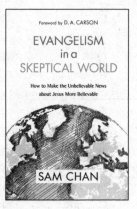

Most Christians already know they should be telling their friends about Jesus. But they have been poorly equipped with methods that are no longer effective in today's post-Christian world. As a result, many people become frustrated, blame themselves, and simply give up. *Evangelism in a Skeptical World* is a textbook on evangelism that is ideal for the church or the classroom to equip Christians with the principles and skills they need to tell the unbelievable news about Jesus to friends in a skeptical world.

Many of the older principles and methods of evangelism in the twentieth century no longer work effectively today. In a post-Christian, post-churched, post-reached world, we need new methods to communicate the timeless message of the gospel in culturally relevant ways.

Dr. Chan combines the theological and biblical insights of classic evangelistic training with the latest insights from missiology on contextualization, cultural hermeneutics, and storytelling. Every chapter is illustrated with real-world examples drawn from more than fifteen years of evangelistic ministry. These are methods that really work—with university students, urban workers, and professionals—to get past the defensive posture that people have toward Christianity so they can seriously consider the claims of Jesus Christ.

Field-tested and filled with unique, fresh, and creative insights, this book will equip you to share the gospel in today's world and help as many people as possible hear the good news about Jesus.

Available in stores and online!